Elements of Literature®

Fourth Course

Holt Adapted Reader

Instruction in Reading Literature and Informational Texts

HOLT, RINEHART AND WINSTON

A Harcourt Education Company

Orlando • **Austin** • New York • San Diego • Toronto • London

9 179 09 08 07

Contents

Skills Table of Contents

PHOTO CREDITS

To the Student

Imagine this: a book full of great stories and interesting informational texts. Make it a book that actually tells you to write in it. Fill it with graphic organizers that encourage you to think a different way. Make it a size that's easy to carry around. That's *Holt Adapted Reader*—a book created especially for you.

In *Holt Adapted Reader* you will find two kinds of selections—original literature and adaptations. Original literature is exactly what appears in *Elements of Literature*, Fourth Course. All the poems and plays in this book are examples of original literature.

Adaptations are based on stories or articles that appear in *Elements of Literature*, Fourth Course. Adaptations make the selections more accessible to all readers. You can easily identify any selection that is an adaptation. Just look for the words *based on* in the Table of Contents.

Learning to Read Literary and Informational Texts

When you read informational texts like a social studies textbook or a newspaper article, you usually read to get the facts. You read mainly to get information that is stated directly on the page. When you read literature, you need to go beyond the words on the page. You need to read between the lines of a poem or story to discover the writer's meaning. No matter what kind of reading you do, *Holt Adapted Reader* will help you practice the skills and strategies you need to become an active and successful reader.

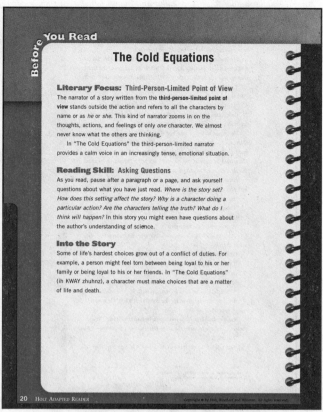

Before You Read

The Cold Equations

Literary Focus: Third-Person-Limited Point of View
The narrator of a story written from the **third-person-limited point of view** stands outside the action and refers to all the characters by name or as *he* or *she*. This kind of narrator zooms in on the thoughts, actions, and feelings of only *one* character. We almost never know what the others are thinking.

In "The Cold Equations" the third-person-limited narrator provides a calm voice in an increasingly tense, emotional situation.

Reading Skill: Asking Questions
As you read, pause after a paragraph or a page, and ask yourself questions about what you have just read. *Where is the story set? How does this setting affect the story? Why is a character doing a particular action? Are the characters telling the truth? What do I think will happen?* In this story you might even have questions about the author's understanding of science.

Into the Story
Some of life's hardest choices grow out of a conflict of duties. For example, a person might feel torn between being loyal to his or her family or being loyal to his or her friends. In "The Cold Equations" (ih KWAY zhuhnz), a character must make choices that are a matter of life and death.

Before You Read

On the **Before You Read** page you will preview the two skills you will practice as you read the selection.

- In the **Literary Focus** you will learn about one literary element—such as character or rhyme. This literary element is one you will see in the selection.
- The **Reading Skill** presents a key skill that you will learn and practice as you read the selection.

The **Before You Read** page also introduces you to the reading selection.

- **Into the Story** (or another genre) gives you background information. This information will help you understand the selection or its author. It may also help you understand the time period in which the selection was written.

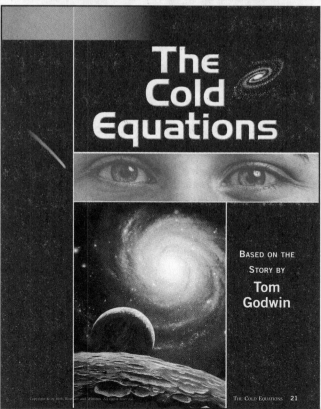

The Cold Equations

BASED ON THE STORY BY **Tom Godwin**

Interactive Selections from *Elements of Literature*

Many of the readings in this book are the same ones that appear in *Elements of Literature,* Fourth Course. Some are adaptations of selections in *Elements of Literature.* The selections are printed to give you room to mark up the text.

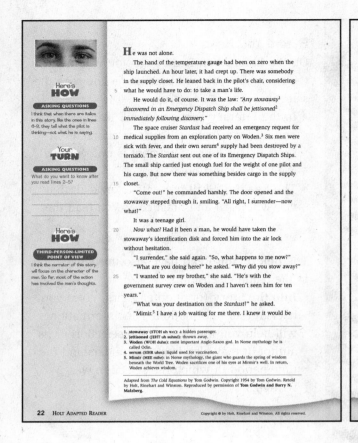

Here's HOW

ASKING QUESTIONS

I think that when there are italics in this story, like the ones in lines 6–8, they tell what the pilot is thinking—not what he is saying.

Your TURN

ASKING QUESTIONS

What do you want to know after you read lines 2–5?

_____

_____

Here's HOW

THIRD-PERSON-LIMITED POINT OF VIEW

I think the narrator of this story will focus on the character of the man. So far, most of the action has involved the man's thoughts.

He was not alone.

The hand of the temperature gauge had been on zero when the ship launched. An hour later, it had crept up. There was somebody in the supply closet. He leaned back in the pilot's chair, considering what he would have to do: to take a man's life.

5 He would do it, of course. It was the law: "*Any stowaway*[1] *discovered in an Emergency Dispatch Ship shall be jettisoned*[2] *immediately following discovery.*"

The space cruiser *Stardust* had received an emergency request for medical supplies from an exploration party on Woden.[3] Six men were
10 sick with fever, and their own serum[4] supply had been destroyed by a tornado. The *Stardust* sent out one of its Emergency Dispatch Ships. The small ship carried just enough fuel for the weight of one pilot and his cargo. But now there was something besides cargo in the supply
15 closet.

"Come out!" he commanded harshly. The door opened and the stowaway stepped through it, smiling. "All right, I surrender—now what?"

It was a teenage girl.

20 *Now what?* Had it been a man, he would have taken the stowaway's identification disk and forced him into the air lock without hesitation.

"I surrender," she said again. "So, what happens to me now?"

"What are you doing here?" he asked. "Why did you stow away?"

25 "I wanted to see my brother," she said. "He's with the government survey crew on Woden and I haven't seen him for ten years."

"What was your destination on the *Stardust*?" he asked.

"Mimir.[5] I have a job waiting for me there. I knew it would be

---

1. **stowaway** (STOH uh way): a hidden passenger.
2. **jettisoned** (JEHT uh suhnd): thrown away.
3. **Woden** (WOH duhn): most important Anglo-Saxon god. In Norse mythology he is called Odin.
4. **serum** (SIHR uhm): liquid used for vaccination.
5. **Mimir** (MEE mihr): in Norse mythology, the giant who guards the spring of wisdom beneath the World Tree. Woden sacrifices one of his eyes at Mimir's well. In return, Woden achieves wisdom.

Adapted from *The Cold Equations* by Tom Godwin. Copyright 1954 by Tom Godwin. Retold by Holt, Rinehart and Winston. Reproduced by permission of **Tom Godwin and Barry N. Malzberg.**

---

30 almost a year before Gerry's job was done on Woden. I didn't want to wait another year when I could see him now."

She could not be blamed for her ignorance of the law. Yet there had been a sign over the door that led to the section of the *Stardust* that housed the EDSs: UNAUTHORIZED PERSONNEL KEEP OUT!
35 There were two different survey groups on Woden, so he asked, "What is your brother's name?"

"Cross—Gerry Cross. He's in Group Two," she said.

Group One had requested the serum. Group Two was eight thousand miles away, across the Western Sea.
40 He turned to the control board and cut the deceleration to a fraction of a gravity, knowing as he did so that it could not change the ending. Then he turned the switch that would signal the *Stardust*. The call would be useless, but he could not bring himself to force her into the air lock as he would an animal—or a man.
45 A voice spoke from the communicator. "*Stardust*. Identify yourself and proceed."

"Barton, EDS 34GII. Emergency. Give me Commander Delhart."

"Barton?" The commander barked from the communicator. "What's this about an emergency?"
50 "A stowaway," he answered.

"A stowaway? That's unusual—but why the 'emergency' call?" asked Delhart.

"The stowaway is a girl," Barton replied.

"I see." The sharpness was gone from the commander's voice.
55 "I'm sorry—I can do nothing. You'll have to go through with it."

Barton turned back to the girl, whose eyes were fixed wide.

"What did he mean, to go through with it?" she asked warily.[6]

Her time was too short for the comfort of a lie. "He meant it the way it sounded," he said.
60 She recoiled[7] from him as though he had struck her. "You mean . . . I have to leave the ship? But you can't make me—I'll *die*."

"I know."

"But I didn't do anything to die for—I didn't *do* anything—."

---

6. **warily** (WAIR uh lee): carefully, cautiously.
7. **recoiled** (rih KOYLD): stepped back.

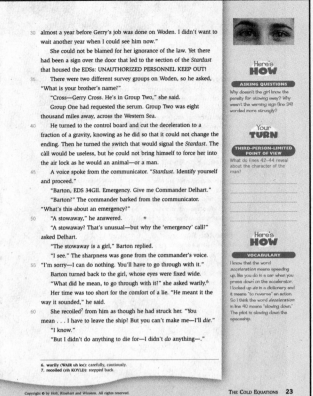

Here's HOW

ASKING QUESTIONS

Why doesn't the girl know the penalty for stowing away? Why wasn't the warning sign (line 34) worded more strongly?

Your TURN

THIRD-PERSON-LIMITED POINT OF VIEW

What do lines 42–44 reveal about the character of the man?

_____

_____

Here's HOW

VOCABULARY

I know that the word *acceleration* means speeding up, like you do in a car when you press down on the accelerator. I looked up *de* in a dictionary and it means "to reverse" an action. So I think the word *deceleration* in line 40 means "slowing down." The pilot is slowing down the spaceship.

Here's HOW

The **Here's HOW** feature models, or shows you, how to apply a particular skill to what you are reading. This feature lets you see how another person might think about the text. Each **Here's HOW** focuses on a reading skill, a literary skill, or a vocabulary skill. You can tell the focus of a **Here's HOW** by looking in the green oval under the heading.

Your TURN

The **Your TURN** feature gives you a chance to practice a skill on your own. Each **Your TURN** focuses on a reading skill, a literary skill, or a vocabulary skill. You might be asked to underline or circle words in the text. You might also be asked to write your response to a question on lines that are provided for you.

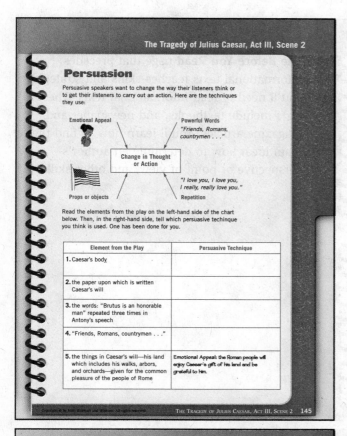

Graphic Organizers

After each selection is a **graphic organizer.** These organizers give you another way to understand the reading skill or literary focus of the selection. You might be asked to chart the main events of the plot or complete a cause-and-effect chart.

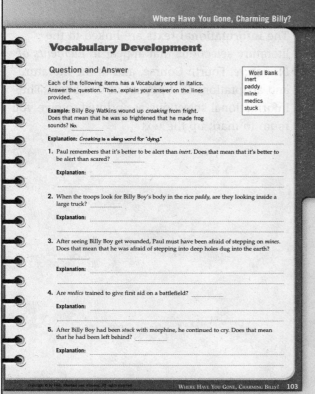

Vocabulary Development

Vocabulary Development worksheets appear at the end of some literary selections. These worksheets help you develop skills for building vocabulary.

Reading Informational Texts

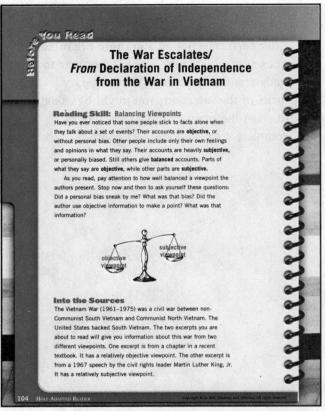

Before You Read
The **Before You Read** page that precedes informational texts teaches skills and strategies you'll need to read informational texts. These texts include textbooks, and newspaper and magazine articles. You'll learn how to find the main idea, how to determine an author's perspective or point of view, and other skills.

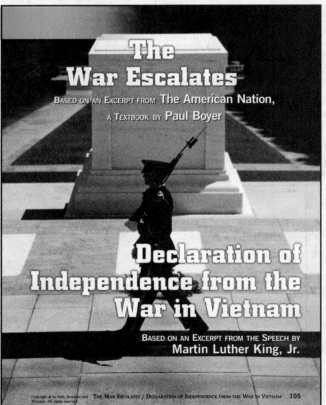

Interactive Informational Texts
The **informational texts** are linked to the literature selections that appear in *Elements of Literature,* Fourth Course, and to the literature and adaptations that appear in this book. The informational selections are printed to give you room to mark up the text.

Johnson claimed that the Communists had attacked first. The truth is, the U.S. destroyer *Maddox* had fired first. The second attack may never have happened. Some U.S. sailors apparently had misread their radar. But Johnson and his advisers got what they wanted: the power to expand the war.

By passing the resolution, Congress gave up its power to declare war. As Senator Wayne Morse pointed out, "We are in effect giving the President war-making powers in the absence of a declaration of war."

U.S. Forces in Vietnam

President Johnson soon called for an escalation, or buildup, of U.S. forces. In April 1965, more than 13,000 young men were drafted to serve in the armed forces.

The troops. More than 2 million Americans served in Vietnam. At first, most were professional soldiers who had enlisted. Later, more draftees were shipped to Vietnam. The average U.S. soldier in Vietnam was younger than those who had served in World War II or the Korean War. He was also poorer and had less education.

Young men from families with higher incomes were least likely to serve in Vietnam. They got deferments, postponements of service, mostly because they were going to college.

African Americans and Hispanics served in combat in very high numbers. In 1965 almost 24 percent of all battle deaths were African American. Yet they made up just 11 percent of the total number of people in the United States.

Soldiers in Vietnam faced terrible hardships. Some faced the enemy in battles. Others cut their way through jungles. They heard but did not see the enemy. Others searched house to house for enemy soldiers. Most Americans served in support jobs. But no one who served in Vietnam was safe. Rockets could strike anywhere.

Some 10,000 servicewomen had noncombat jobs in Vietnam, mostly as nurses. They faced the horrors of war daily. Another 20,000 to 45,000 women worked as civilians for groups such as the Red Cross.

Here's HOW

VOCABULARY

I'm not sure what *escalation* means in line 36. Maybe it's related to *escalator* and means something that moves up? Yeah, that's right. The next word, *buildup*, repeats the meaning of *escalation* in another way. So, an escalation of troops means that the number of soldiers increased, or went up.

Your TURN

VOCABULARY

Circle any words in lines 44–46 that help you understand what *deferments* means. Then, rewrite lines 44–46 in your own words.

Your TURN

BALANCING VIEWPOINTS

This article began with a typical textbook tone—objective and unbiased. However, in the section "The troops" (lines 39–59), the tone becomes more concerned and critical. Underline words and phrases that show this subjective tone.

THE WAR ESCALATES / DECLARATION OF INDEPENDENCE FROM THE WAR IN VIETNAM   **107**

Side Notes

Notes in the side column accompany each selection. They guide your experience with the text and help you unlock its meaning. Many notes ask you to circle or underline words in the text itself.

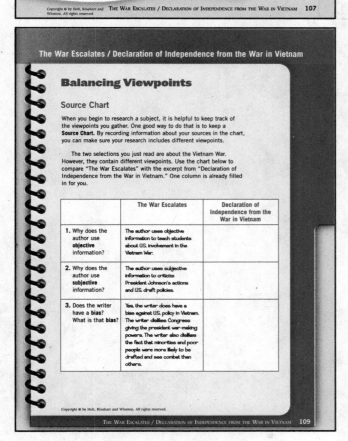

The War Escalates / Declaration of Independence from the War in Vietnam

Balancing Viewpoints

Source Chart

When you begin to research a subject, it is helpful to keep track of the viewpoints you gather. One good way to do that is to keep a **Source Chart**. By recording information about your sources in the chart, you can make sure your research includes different viewpoints.

The two selections you just read are about the Vietnam War. However, they contain different viewpoints. Use the chart below to compare "The War Escalates" with the excerpt from "Declaration of Independence from the War in Vietnam." One column is already filled in for you.

	The War Escalates	Declaration of Independence from the War in Vietnam
1. Why does the author use **objective** information?	The author uses objective information to teach students about U.S. involvement in the Vietnam War.	
2. Why does the author use **subjective** information?	The author uses subjective information to criticize President Johnson's actions and U.S. draft policies.	
3. Does the writer have a **bias**? What is that **bias**?	Yes, the writer does have a bias against U.S. policy in Vietnam. The writer dislikes Congress giving the president war-making powers. The writer also dislikes the fact that minorities and poor people were more likely to be drafted and see combat than others.	

THE WAR ESCALATES / DECLARATION OF INDEPENDENCE FROM THE WAR IN VIETNAM   **109**

Graphic Organizers

After each selection, a **graphic organizer** gives you another way to understand the selection. These organizers focus on the skill introduced on the Before You Read page. You might, for example, be asked to collect supporting details that point to a main idea or to complete a comparison chart.

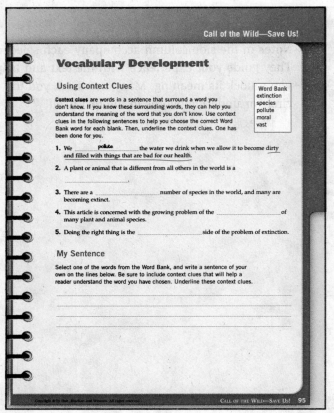

Vocabulary Development

Some informational texts have **Vocabulary Development Worksheets.** These worksheets help you practice your understanding of vocabulary words in exercises like the one shown here.

Holt Adapted Reader

Instruction in Reading Literature and Informational Texts

Diary of a Mad Blender: A Week of Managing Every Spare Minute

Reading Skill: Identifying the Main Idea

The **main idea** is the message, opinion, or insight that is the focus of a piece of nonfiction writing. To find the main idea, look for key statements made by the writer. Look also for supporting details, and think about what the details add up to. Does the writer support ideas with facts, statistics, examples, brief real-life stories, or quotations? Make a chart like the one below to help you identify the writer's main idea and support:

Main Idea 1	Main Idea 2
Support 1	Support 1
Support 2	Support 2

Into the Article

Have you ever had trouble juggling multiple tasks at once? The article you are about to read is an amusing look at how one work-at-home mother tries to combine work and family.

Diary of a Mad Blender:

A Week of Managing Every Spare Minute

BASED ON THE *WALL STREET JOURNAL* ARTICLE BY

Sue Shellenbarger

Here's HOW

IDENTIFYING THE MAIN IDEA

In lines 4–9, the author seems to be indicating that combining work with family time is a challenge. This idea is supported by the story about how the author has trouble focusing on work-related issues when she goes snowboarding with her kids.

Your TURN

IDENTIFYING THE MAIN IDEA

How do the events in lines 10–26 support the idea that combining family with work is difficult for the author?

_____

_____

_____

_____

It's one of the hottest work-life trends: integrating work and personal roles. So I bought an armload of time-management and life-balance books and tried some of their tips.

- **Friday.** To mix some play with my work, I quit my office a
5   couple of hours early. I pack my cell phone and laptop and drive my kids to a nearby ski area for a little night snowboarding. As I help my son with his bindings, a co-worker calls on my cell phone to ask for sources for a story. Though I know the subject, I draw a blank.

10 - **Monday.** The experts suggest a list of things to do while my computer is booting up. I love one bit of advice: Write a postcard to a friend. However, when I try taking a "minivacation," closing my eyes and breathing deep, I can't seem to relax.

I pick up voice mail on my cell phone while driving my
15   kids home from school and listen to a time-management book on tape. Though I get it all done, my brain feels like L.A. after an earthquake.

- **Tuesday.** *In Take Back Your Time,* Jan Jasper advises getting little tasks done while watching TV. I try opening mail and sorting
20   work papers. I make a big dent in my office piles. But my daughter, who usually looks forward to watching TV with me, leaves the room.

- **Wednesday.** My experiment has indeed made me more efficient. My office is neater. I'm embracing some of the tips permanently,
25   such as taking work with me to do while waiting in doctors' offices.

From "Diary of a Mad Blender: A Week of Managing Every Spare Minute" by Sue Shellenbarger adapted from *The Wall Street Journal,* March 22, 2000. Copyright © 2000 by Dow Jones & Company, Inc. Retold by Holt, Rinehart and Winston. Reproduced by permission **The Wall Street Journal.**

But jugglers beware. It was far easier for me to splice more work into my week than to add time for rest and relationships. And the more I cram into my days, the stupider I get.

30   Maybe my brain just needs a little cross-training. But in its current condition, it clearly needs a good long rest.

Seeing the Big Picture

The **main idea** is the message, opinion, or insight that is the focus of a piece of nonfiction writing. Fill in the main-idea chart below with supporting details from the article you've just read. These details will lead you to the main idea.

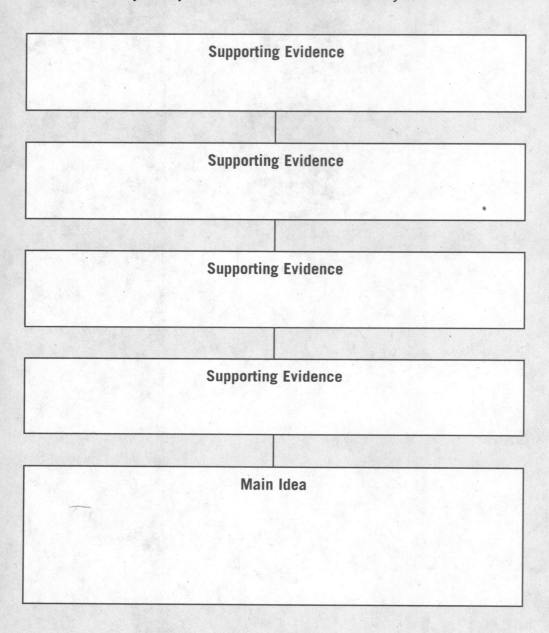

Supporting Evidence

Supporting Evidence

Supporting Evidence

Supporting Evidence

Main Idea

Vocabulary Development

Analogies

In an **analogy** question the words in the first pair relate to each other in the same way that the words in the second pair do. Follow the steps below when you complete an analogy question:

DARK : LIGHT :: _____ : expensive

    a. dear   **b.** cheap   **c.** costly   **d.** bright

1. Identify the relationship between the words in the first pair. (In the example above, *dark* and *light* are opposites, or antonyms.)

2. Express the analogy in sentence or question form. (Dark *is the opposite of* light, *just as* _____ *is the opposite of* expensive.)

3. From the choices available, choose the word that makes the second relationship the same as the first. (Look for a word that means the opposite of *expensive*. Choice b, *cheap*, is correct.)

The following chart shows some of the relationships you'll find in analogy test items and gives an example for each:

Type of Relationship	Example
Synonyms	QUICK : FAST :: loud : noisy
Antonyms	ENTER : DEPART :: build : destroy
Part of something to the whole	TOE : FOOT :: roof : house
Thing/object to the category it belongs to	ROBIN : BIRD :: maple : tree
Thing to a characteristic of the thing	BASEBALL : ROUND :: silk : smooth
Degree of intensity	GOOD : GREAT :: thin : emaciated
Worker to a tool the worker uses	PAINTER : BRUSH :: plumber : wrench

Identify the type of relationship in each of the following word pairs:

1. keyboard : laptop

2. labrador : dog

3. children : young

4. writer : computer

A Baby's Quilt to Sew Up the Generations

Reading Skill: Understanding Secondary Sources.
The materials you find when researching historical information can generally be put into two categories: primary sources and secondary sources.

- A **primary source** is original material, a firsthand account of information that has not been interpreted or edited by other writers. Oral histories, autobiographies, letters, and speeches are primary sources.

- A **secondary source** is based on other sources. It contains information that is at least one step removed from an event and is usually retold, interpreted, or summarized by the writer. Encyclopedia articles and most magazine articles are secondary sources; so are biographies, textbooks, reference books, and literary criticism. Most newspaper articles are secondary sources.

Using the Sources

The following steps can help you use the information in a secondary source to learn about a topic:

- **Analyze.** Read the material carefully. Who is the speaker or writer, and who is the intended audience? What is the message, or **main idea**? What details support the main idea?

- **Evaluate.** How accurate is the message? Do you agree with the writer's message? Look for clues that tell you if you are reading **opinions** or **facts.**

- **Elaborate.** When doing research, you'll want to elaborate on the information you find in your sources. When you **elaborate,** you add something, usually more details. You might offer your own ideas on the topic, or you might do further research.

Into the Article

Quilting has long been an important folk art and cultural tradition in America. This secondary source explains the origins of one family quilt.

A Baby's Quilt to Sew Up the Generations

BASED ON THE *NEW YORK TIMES* ARTICLE BY

Felicia R. Lee

Here's
HOW

**UNDERSTANDING
SECONDARY SOURCES**

In lines 8–10, the writer says that
we live in a time when many
families are broken up. This
seems like an accurate statement
based on the divorce rate in this
country.

Your
TURN

**UNDERSTANDING
SECONDARY SOURCES**

Based on what the writer says
in the last paragraph, what is
the main idea of this article?
Which details in the article
support this main idea?

_____

_____

_____

The stepgrandparents on the mother's side sent a photo of
themselves in Pisa, Italy. Cousin Barbara sent a quotation from a
classic children's book. . . . From a . . . great-great-grandmother came
a piece of her apron. On it was written a cookie recipe.

5   Each contribution was attached to a fabric square. Each is part of
a quilt that Marilyn Webb, a New York writer . . . , is making for her
first grandchild. . . .

The quilt . . . is draped over a couch in Ms. Webb's dining room.
It is an old-fashioned gift for a new kind of family. It is a family story
10 . . . stitched together at a time when so many families drift apart. . . .

. . . Ms. Webb sent a letter to dozens of family members. It read,
in part: ". . . I'd like to make this new baby a welcome quilt in which
he or she can be wrapped in the very fabric of our families' lives. A
true family quilt and maybe a new family tradition."

15   . . . She asked family members to write a letter introducing
themselves to the new child and telling . . . what was special about
their seven-inch squares.

In this way, the pieces of lives came by mail from all over the
country. Ms. Webb received scraps of tablecloths, shirts, baby
20 blankets, bibs.

Some of the pieces came from people connected to the baby by
blood. Some came from people linked by marriage.

Ms. Webb used books to teach herself to make a quilt. She turned
her dining room into a sewing room.

25   She believes quilting is an idea for these times, as many people
are seeking ways to have more family time and preserve family
history.

From "A Baby's Quilt to Sew Up the Generations" by Felicia R. Lee adapted from *The New
York Times*, July 9, 2000. Copyright © 2000 by **The New York Times Agency.** Retold by Holt,
Rinehart and Winston. Reproduced by the publisher.

Source Quilt

A quilt is made up of scraps of cloth that, when sewn together, create something useful and beautiful. Similarly, a report or article is made up of bits of information that, when put together, inform or entertain us.

Use the following "source quilt" to come up with ideas for an article you might write about a local event from your town's recent or distant past. Fill in each box with a source that you'd explore for the article. Then, circle what kind of source it is—primary or secondary (look back at page 8 for help in identifying sources). The first box has been filled in for you.

EVENT: _____

Source: history of town written by local historian primary or (secondary)	**Source:** diary entry from town resident (primary) or secondary
Source: _____ primary or secondary	**Source:** _____ primary or secondary

By Any Other Name

Literary Focus: Character and Autobiography

Fiction writers often use **indirect characterization** to create characters that seem real. This means that they *show* rather than *tell* what their characters look like and what they say, do, and think. So how does a nonfiction writer (in this case a writer of **autobiography**) reveal what her real-life characters are like? Notice how Santha Rama Rau brings her characters and their conflicts to life. Are her techniques the same as those of fiction writers, or are they different?

Reading Skill: Comparison and Contrast

When you **compare** people or things, you show their similarities—how they are alike. When you **contrast** people or things, you show how they are different. When the sisters in this account enroll in a school in their native India that is run by teachers from England, they encounter cultural differences. As you read, compare and contrast these two cultures and the different attitudes the two sisters have toward them.

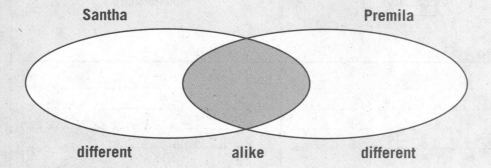

Santha   Premila

different   alike   different

Into the Autobiography

At the time of this account (around 1928), India was a colony of Great Britain. Educated Indians were expected to learn English in addition to their native languages. The headmistress of Rama Rau's school is British, as are most of the students.

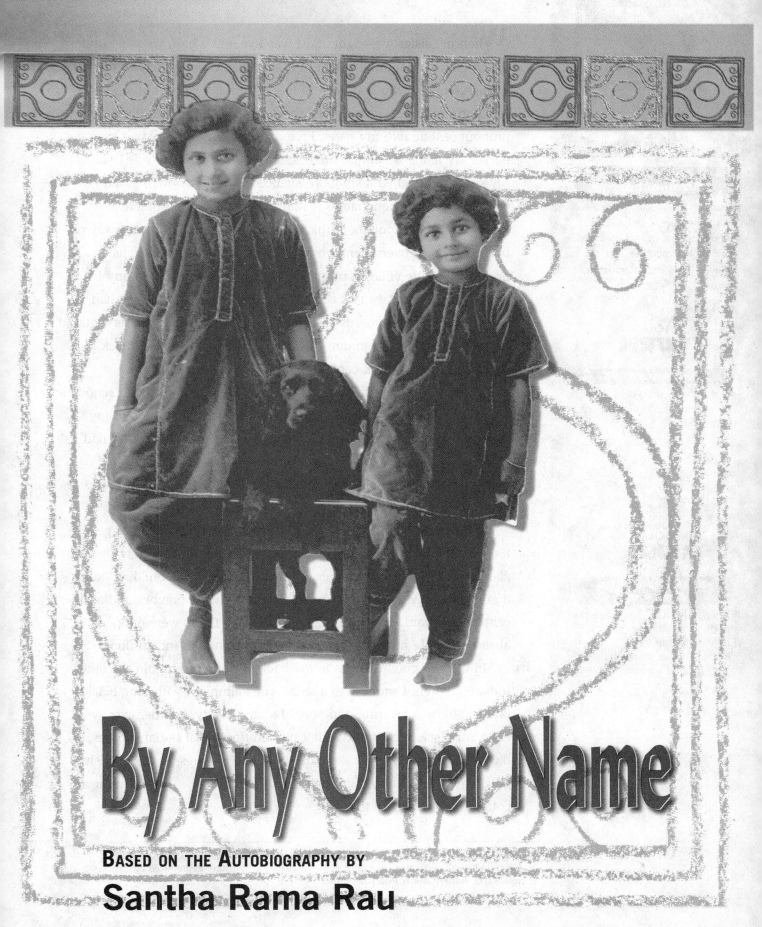

By Any Other Name

BASED ON THE AUTOBIOGRAPHY BY

Santha Rama Rau

Here's HOW

CHARACTER AND AUTOBIOGRAPHY

Based on the information in the first paragraph, I can tell that the principal of the school looks down on Indian culture and believes that her own culture is better.

Your TURN

VOCABULARY

What clue in lines 22–25 helps you figure out the meaning of the word *dual* in line 25?

_____

_____

_____

Your TURN

COMPARISON AND CONTRAST

Re-read lines 28–34. What are the differences between the English children and the Indian children at the school? Is one group favored over another? Explain.

_____

_____

_____

_____

When my sister was eight and I was five and a half, we were sent to a British school in our town in India. The school principal was an English woman who had been in India for many years, but when we told her our names, she insisted they were much too hard for her to
5 pronounce. She told my sister, Premila, that Pamela would be her new name. My name is Santha; the best she could do for me was Cynthia. My sister maintained a stubborn silence when the woman asked how we felt about our new names. I said "Thank you" very quietly.

We started school about this time because my father was away on
10 business. As a government worker, he had to make inspections on horseback in the villages around our little country town. So on one of the hot, windless days that comes before the rainy season, we had waved goodbye to him, his assistant, his secretary, and two servants. As they rode off through our garden, my sister and I turned back to
15 the shade of the house, cooled by fans in every room.

So far, my mother had refused to send Premila to a British school. No matter how long English people lived in India, it seemed to my mother that they never adapted to India. So far too, my mother had taken care of our education herself. But now her good health had
20 broken down, so we put away our books and left our Indian stories behind.

The first day of school was remarkable. Having two names gave me a kind of split personality. As I followed the principal to my classroom, I felt like a stranger to "Cynthia." Even the building had a
25 dual personality. Like Indian buildings, it had wide porches and a central courtyard, but like British schools, the floors were dark, absorbing more heat than the whitewashed stone of Indian floors.

In the classroom, I went to the back of the room to join the other Indian children. I sat next to a small, unsmiling girl with long black
30 braids. She was wearing traditional Indian jewelry, and her eyes were edged in black like mine. While I had on traditional Indian clothes, though, she was wearing a cotton dress like the dresses the English girls wore. Right away, I decided to ask my mother if I could wear a cotton dress to school too.

"By Any Other Name" adapted from *Gifts of Passage* by Santha Rama Rau. Copyright © 1961 by Vasanthi Rama Rau Bowers. Retold by Holt, Rinehart and Winston. Reproduced by permission of **HarperCollins Publishers, Inc.**

35 When the teacher asked me to say my name to the class that morning, I didn't say anything. She frowned and asked again, "What's your name?" I hesitated and then said, "I don't know." The English children giggled and stared at me. The little girl with the braids touched my arm as if she understood my confusion.

40 I was bored in school that day, so I spent my time watching a lizard on the ledge of a high window behind the teacher. My mother had already taught me most of what was in the teacher's lessons. Only the word "apple" was new.

At lunch, I followed the girl with braids out to the covered porch,
45 then ran to join Premila, who had our shared lunchbox. We were the only ones who had Indian food. Embarrassed, Premila shoved my share at me and whispered angrily that I should go sit with the girls my age, as the others were doing. The girl with braids looked at my food as if she were very hungry, but when I offered her some, she
50 shook her head and ate her sandwiches instead.

It was hard to stay awake after lunch. At home, we took naps in our bedroom, shaded against the hot afternoon sun. We drifted off to the sound of my mother's voice reading and woke up when the maid woke us for tea. At school, though, we rested briefly on cots and then
55 played games, staying indoors until the shadows and the evening breeze made it possible to play outdoors.

I had a hard time with the games we played. At home, I was allowed to win because I was the youngest, but since I didn't have to compete to win, I didn't really understand what winning meant or
60 how to go about trying to do it. At school on that first day, I let one of the English boys catch me at tag, but then I didn't understand why the others wouldn't let me catch them. When our maid arrived to take us home, I raced to the car, shouting her name. It seemed like forever since morning, when she had told me repeatedly how to be a good
65 girl at school. Premila was embarrassed at my running; she told me never to do it again in front of the other children.

At home, we went straight to my mother's room to have tea with her. When she asked me about school, nothing else occurred to me, so I told her what "apple" meant. Premila told Mother that she would

VOCABULARY

I looked up the word *hesitated* (line 37) in a dictionary and found out that it means "paused or delayed in acting."

CHARACTER AND AUTOBIOGRAPHY

Re-read lines 44–50. What have you learned about Premila's character so far?

_____

_____

_____

COMPARISON AND CONTRAST

Lines 57–62 reveal that the English children value competing in games and winning. Santha and her family, on the other hand, seem to value helping other players—even if they're opponents.

COMPARISON AND CONTRAST

According to lines 67–73, how are Santha and Premila different?

_____

_____

_____

VOCABULARY

What clue in lines 83–85 helps you figure out the meaning of the word *abruptly* in line 77?

_____

_____

_____

Here's **HOW**

VOCABULARY

I can figure out that the word *deserted* (line 91) means "empty" because only "a few people were out."

CHARACTER AND AUTOBIOGRAPHY

What does the incident in lines 94–103 reveal about Premila's character?

_____

_____

_____

70 have weekly tests, and when I asked what a test was, my sister told me that I was too young to need to know. She also told Mother that we should take sandwiches to school the next day, covering her own embarrassment by saying that sandwiches would be simpler for me.

That evening I had so much fun playing outdoors with the cook's
75 son that I didn't even think about school. When the maid came to hurry me into supper, I was happy to be back in my usual routine.

A week later, our lives changed abruptly. Already, I had fallen into a routine, sitting in the back of the room and letting my mind wander. I was getting to know Nalini, the girl with braids; the school had
80 renamed her Natalie. We sometimes drew pictures and showed them to each other. As young as I was, I knew that being friends with the English or Anglo-Indian children was not possible for us.

When the door opened suddenly and Premila marched in, the teacher smiled and tried to speak to her. Ignoring her, Premila told me
85 to get up. "We're going home," she said. I was confused, but when she told me to get my pencils and notebooks, I obeyed. On the way home, when I asked what was wrong, my sister just said, "We're going home for good."

It was a very tiring walk, and the heat of the day made it seem
90 endless to me. A few people were out, but because of the heat, the road was almost deserted. I lagged behind Premila, whining at her to wait for me. She said nothing, except for telling me to shade my head by carrying my notebook on it.

When we arrived at home, it was time for lunch. The maid
95 wondered why we were home in the middle of the day, and my mother immediately asked Premila to explain what was wrong. Premila explained that since it was test day, her teacher had put her Indian students at the back of the room, with empty desks between the students. The teacher explained that she was separating the Indian
100 students this way because otherwise they would cheat. Premila finished her story by saying that we should not go back to the British school. My mother agreed. She was clearly not pleased with what had happened to us.

Afterward, we had lunch together, and then I had my nap. Before
105 I fell asleep, I could hear my mother ask Premila if she thought I had
understood her story. Premila didn't think so; she thought I was too
young. Of course, I had understood. But it was easy to put my British
school experience behind me. It didn't feel like it had happened to me
anyway. It had happened to someone named Cynthia.

Characterization

The process through which a writer reveals the personality of a character is called **characterization.** A writer can reveal a character in the following ways:

1. By telling us directly what the character is like

2. By describing how the character looks and dresses

3. By letting us hear the character speak

4. By revealing the character's private thoughts and feelings

5. By showing how other characters feel or behave toward the character.

6. By showing the character's actions

The first method of revealing a character is called **direct characterization.** When a writer uses this method, we do not have to figure out what a character's personality is like—the writer tells us directly. The other five methods of revealing a character are known as **indirect characterization.** When a writer uses these methods, we have to put clues together to figure out what a character is like.

Review the autobiography you've just read, and, using the chart below, gather details about the author, Santha Rama Rau. Briefly explain what these details reveal about her character, and then explain the methods of characterization that she has used.

Details About Santha Rama Rau	What These Details Reveal	Methods of Characterization

Vocabulary Development

Putting Words in Context

Word Bank
dual
hesitated
abruptly
deserted

Organize what you know about each of the three remaining words in the Word Bank by making a cluster diagram like the one below for *deserted*. Brainstorm to come up with several questions that suggest **contexts** in which each word is used correctly. Then, list words or phrases that answer your questions.

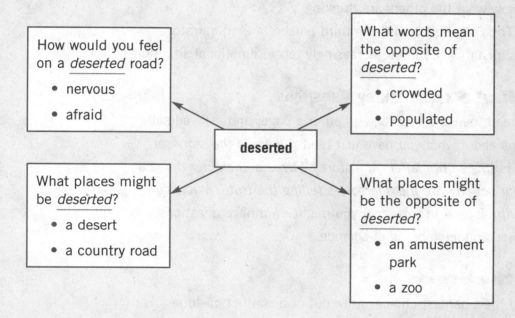

How would you feel on a *deserted* road?
- nervous
- afraid

What words mean the opposite of *deserted*?
- crowded
- populated

deserted

What places might be *deserted*?
- a desert
- a country road

What places might be the opposite of *deserted*?
- an amusement park
- a zoo

The Cold Equations

Literary Focus: Third-Person-Limited Point of View

The narrator of a story written from the **third-person-limited point of view** stands outside the action and refers to all the characters by name or as *he* or *she*. This kind of narrator zooms in on the thoughts, actions, and feelings of only *one* character. We almost never know what the others are thinking.

In "The Cold Equations" the third-person-limited narrator provides a calm voice in an increasingly tense, emotional situation.

Reading Skill: Asking Questions

As you read, pause after a paragraph or a page, and ask yourself questions about what you have just read. *Where is the story set? How does this setting affect the story? Why is a character doing a particular action? Are the characters telling the truth? What do I think will happen?* In this story you might even have questions about the author's understanding of science.

Into the Story

Some of life's hardest choices grow out of a conflict of duties. For example, a person might feel torn between being loyal to his or her family or being loyal to his or her friends. In "The Cold Equations" (ih KWAY zhuhnz), a character must make choices that are a matter of life and death.

The Cold Equations

BASED ON THE STORY BY **Tom Godwin**

He was not alone.

The hand of the temperature gauge had been on zero when the ship launched. An hour later, it had crept up. There was somebody in the supply closet. He leaned back in the pilot's chair, considering
5 what he would have to do: to take a man's life.

He would do it, of course. It was the law: *"Any stowaway[1] discovered in an Emergency Dispatch Ship shall be jettisoned[2] immediately following discovery."*

The space cruiser *Stardust* had received an emergency request for
10 medical supplies from an exploration party on Woden.[3] Six men were sick with fever, and their own serum[4] supply had been destroyed by a tornado. The *Stardust* sent out one of its Emergency Dispatch Ships. The small ship carried just enough fuel for the weight of one pilot and his cargo. But now there was something besides cargo in the supply
15 closet.

"Come out!" he commanded harshly. The door opened and the stowaway stepped through it, smiling. "All right, I surrender—now what?"

It was a teenage girl.

20 *Now what?* Had it been a man, he would have taken the stowaway's identification disk and forced him into the air lock without hesitation.

"I surrender," she said again. "So, what happens to me now?"

"What are you doing here?" he asked. "Why did you stow away?"

25 "I wanted to see my brother," she said. "He's with the government survey crew on Woden and I haven't seen him for ten years."

"What was your destination on the *Stardust*?" he asked.

"Mimir.[5] I have a job waiting for me there. I knew it would be

---

1. **stowaway** (STOH uh WAY): a hidden passenger.
2. **jettisoned** (JEHT uh suhnd): thrown away.
3. **Woden** (WOH duhn): most important Anglo-Saxon god. In Norse mythology he is called Odin.
4. **serum** (SIHR uhm): liquid used for vaccination.
5. **Mimir** (MEE mihr): in Norse mythology, the giant who guards the spring of wisdom beneath the World Tree. Woden sacrifices one of his eyes at Mirmir's well. In return, Woden achieves wisdom.

Adapted from *The Cold Equations* by Tom Godwin. Copyright 1954 by Tom Godwin. Retold by Holt, Rinehart and Winston. Reproduced by permission of **Tom Godwin and Barry N. Malzberg**.

30 almost a year before Gerry's job was done on Woden. I didn't want to wait another year when I could see him now."

She could not be blamed for her ignorance of the law. Yet there had been a sign over the door that led to the section of the *Stardust* that housed the EDSs: UNAUTHORIZED PERSONNEL KEEP OUT!

35 There were two different survey groups on Woden, so he asked, "What is your brother's name?"

"Cross—Gerry Cross. He's in Group Two," she said.

Group One had requested the serum. Group Two was eight thousand miles away, across the Western Sea.

40 He turned to the control board and cut the deceleration to a fraction of a gravity, knowing as he did so that it could not change the ending. Then he turned the switch that would signal the *Stardust*. The call would be useless, but he could not bring himself to force her into the air lock as he would an animal—or a man.

45 A voice spoke from the communicator. "*Stardust*. Identify yourself and proceed."

"Barton, EDS 34GII. Emergency. Give me Commander Delhart."

"Barton?" The commander barked from the communicator. "What's this about an emergency?"

50 "A stowaway," he answered.

"A stowaway? That's unusual—but why the 'emergency' call?" asked Delhart.

"The stowaway is a girl," Barton replied.

"I see." The sharpness was gone from the commander's voice.

55 "I'm sorry—I can do nothing. You'll have to go through with it."

Barton turned back to the girl, whose eyes were fixed wide.

"What did he mean, to go through with it?" she asked warily.[6]

Her time was too short for the comfort of a lie. "He meant it the way it sounded," he said.

60 She recoiled[7] from him as though he had struck her. "You mean . . . I have to leave the ship? But you can't make me—I'll *die*."

"I know."

"But I didn't do anything to die for—I didn't *do* anything—."

---

6. **warily** (WAIR uh lee): carefully, cautiously.
7. **recoiled** (rih KOYLD): stepped back.

THE COLD EQUATIONS   **23**

ASKING QUESTIONS

Why doesn't the girl know the penalty for stowing away? Why wasn't the warning sign (line 34) worded more strongly?

THIRD-PERSON-LIMITED POINT OF VIEW

What do lines 42–44 reveal about the character of the man?

_____

_____

_____

_____

VOCABULARY

I know that the word *acceleration* means speeding up, like you do in a car when you press down on the accelerator. I looked up *de* in a dictionary and it means "to reverse" an action. So I think the word *deceleration* in line 40 means "slowing down." The pilot is slowing down the spaceship.

"You'll never know how sorry I am," he said. "It has to be that way and no human can change it."

"EDS," the communicator broke in, "this is Ship's Records. Give us all information on subject's identification disk."

She fumbled with the disk from her necklace; he unfastened it for her.

"Here's your data, Records: Number T8374 dash Y54. Name, Marilyn Lee Cross. Sex, female. Born July 7, 2160." *She was only eighteen.* He turned once again to the girl.

Her childlike voice sounded frightened and bewildered. "Everybody wants me dead, and I didn't *do* anything. I only wanted to see my brother."

"Listen," he said, "nobody would let it be this way if it was possible to change it."

"Then why is it?" she asked.

Barton explained his mission. "This ship has barely enough fuel to get where it's going, and if you stay aboard, your added weight will make it use up all its fuel. It will crash, and you and I will die and so will the six men waiting for the fever serum."

"But isn't there any hope at all that someone, somewhere, could do something to help me?"

"No," he answered. "There are no other cruisers[8] within forty light-years."

"Barton." Commander Delhart's voice came abruptly from the communicator. "Did you reduce the deceleration to point ten?"

"Yes," he answered. "I would like to stay at point ten as long as the computers say I can. Will you ask them?"

It was against regulations, but the commander said only, "I'll feed the data to the computers." The communicator fell silent and he and the girl waited in silence. The chronometer read 18:10 when the commander spoke again.

"You will resume deceleration at 19:10."

"Is that when I go?" she asked. He nodded. Then, he reached out and shut off the communicator. It seemed indecent[9] to let others hear what she might say in her last hour.

---

8. **cruisers** (KROO zuhrz): spaceships.
9. **indecent** (ihn DEE suhnt): not right and proper.

"I understand now," she said after ten silent minutes. "I got into
100 something I didn't know anything about, and now I have to pay for
it."

A physical law had stated: *h amount of fuel will not power an EDS
with a mass of m plus x safely to its destination.* No amount of
sympathy for her could alter that law.

105 "But I'm afraid. I'm going to die and nobody *cares*."

"It isn't that no one cares," Barton said. "It's that no one can do
anything to help. We're all fighting alien[10] environments out here;
there is no margin of safety. Men have to pay the penalty for making
mistakes."

***

110 **W**oden was a sphere[11] swimming in space. Soon it would be night
where Group Two was camped. He estimated how much time
remained before the rotation[12] of Woden would put Group Two
beyond the reach of radio. Thirty minutes—and the chronometer
read 18:30.

115 Four thousand miles away, the tornado that came from the
Woden's Western Sea had destroyed half of Camp One's buildings and
all their medical supplies, then dissolved into air again. It had been a
mindless force, obeying the laws of nature. The men of the frontier
understood that natural laws knew neither hatred nor mercy—but
120 how was a girl from Earth to understand?

***

She straightened up in her seat. "Could I write a letter? I want to
write to Mama and Daddy. And could I talk to Gerry over your radio?"

"I'll try to get him," he said.

Gerry Cross was away from camp, a voice told Barton, but he was
125 expected back within an hour.

---

10. **alien** (AYL yuhn): strange.
11. **sphere** (sfihr): having the shape of a ball.
12. **rotation** (roh TAY shuhn): turning around, circling around.

Here's HOW

ASKING QUESTIONS

Why is the writer using the
scientific equation in lines
102–103 to describe the situation
the stowaway is in? It seems
pretty cold-blooded to me. Is
that what the word *cold* means
in the title of the story?

Your TURN

**THIRD-PERSON-LIMITED
POINT OF VIEW**

What tone is conveyed by the
narrator in lines 115–120?

_____

_____

_____

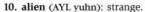

Your TURN

VOCABULARY

The word *range* in line 151 can mean "a Western grassland," "a line of mountains," or "the limits." Which meaning do you think it has here? Explain your answer.

_____

_____

_____

_____

"When he comes in, get him to the transmitter[13] as soon as you possibly can." Barton said; then he turned the volume low and handed her a pad and pencil.

"I'd better write to Gerry too," she said as she took them. "He
130 might not get back to camp in time."

She began to write, a lonely child trying to say her last goodbye; she would tell them how much she loved them and not to feel bad about it. Her brother was a pioneer. He would understand, but her father and mother would not. They would hate Barton. And she
135 would appear in Barton's dreams, to die again. . . .

At 18:45 she folded the second letter and addressed it. "I hope Gerry comes back to camp soon," she said. "I want to hear his voice. I'm a coward and I can't help it."

"No," he said, "you're not a coward. You're afraid, but you're not
140 a coward."

"Is there a difference?" she asked.

He nodded. "A lot of difference."

"Gerry mentioned his work was dangerous, but I didn't understand. I always thought danger along the frontier was an
145 exciting adventure, like in the 3-D shows. Only it's not, is it? Because you can't go home after the show is over."

"No," he said. "You can't."

"I wish Gerry would get back before it's too late," she said.

"I think he will," said Barton, "but there may not be much time
150 left to talk to him before he fades out."

"Then . . . then I'll go when Gerry passes beyond range." She paused and said, "I've caused everyone I love to be hurt, haven't I?"

"It wasn't your fault at all," he said. "They'll understand."

"I keep remembering the little things they did that seem to be the
155 most important to me, now." she said. "Like Gerry—I remember him most for what he did the night my kitten got run over in the street. He held me and told me that Flossy was gone for just a while and would be back the next morning—and she was, just like he had said. Much later Mama told me Gerry got the pet-shop owner out of bed to sell
160 him a white kitten."

---

13. **transmitter** (TRANZ miht uhr): an apparatus that sends out signals.

"It's always the little things we remember," Barton agreed. "You've done things for Gerry and your father and mother that they will never forget."

The signal buzzer interrupted them. Barton spun the volume
165 control knob and asked, "Gerry Cross?"

"Yes," her brother answered tensely. "What is it?"

"Hello, Gerry." There was only a faint quaver[14] in her voice. "I wanted to see you—."

"Marilyn! What are you doing on that EDS?"

170 "I wanted to see you," she said again. "So I stowed away on this ship . . . I didn't know what it would mean—." Then her own composure[15] broke and a tear splashed on his wrist. "Gerry—I only wanted to see you; I didn't intend to hurt you."

"Don't cry, Sis," her brother said gently. " I didn't mean to sound
175 the way I did." Then his voice changed, demanding, "EDS—have you called the *Stardust*?"

"I called the *Stardust* almost an hour ago. It can't turn back," said Barton.

"He tried to help me, Gerry." She had dried her tears. "No one can
180 help me and I'm not going to cry any more and everything will be all right with you and Daddy and Mama, won't it?"

"Sure it will. We'll make out fine," said Gerry.

"You're fading out, Gerry," she said. "We must say goodbye—but maybe I'll see you again. I'll be nothing you can see, but you will
185 know I'm there beside you. Think of me like that, Gerry—always like that."

Only a whisper came back: "Always like that, Marilyn—never any other way."

"Goodbye, Gerry."

190 Faintly, his last words came: "Goodbye, little sister. . . ."

She sat motionless in the hush that followed; then she turned toward the air lock, and he pulled down the black lever beside him. The inner door slid open to reveal a bare cell. She stepped into the air lock and turned to face him.

195 "I'm ready," she said.

---

14. **quaver** (KWAY vuhr): trembling; shaking.
15. **composure** (kuhm POH zhuhr): self-control.

Your
TURN

ASKING QUESTIONS

What questions come to mind when you read that the young girl defends the pilot in line 179?

_____

_____

_____

Here's
HOW

THIRD-PERSON-LIMITED POINT OF VIEW

The narrator describes the actions of Marilyn and Barton (lines 190-199) in a very calm tone. This contrasts with the emotional nature of what is happening. The contrast almost makes the impact of the events on the reader more powerful than if they were described in an excited tone.

Your TURN

VOCABULARY

One meaning of *equation* (line 201) is when something is balanced. What is being balanced, or made equal, in this story?

_____

_____

_____

_____

Your TURN

ASKING QUESTIONS

What questions come to mind when you read the words that echo in the mind of the pilot, "*I didn't do anything to die for*"?

_____

_____

_____

_____

_____

He pushed the lever up and the door slid between them, enclosing her in darkness for her last moments of life. He jerked down the red lever. The ship wavered slightly as the air gushed from the lock. He shoved the red lever back and turned away with slow, heavy steps.

200   He saw that the supply-closet temperature gauge was back on zero. A cold equation had been balanced, and he was alone on the ship. But it seemed, almost, that the girl still sat beside him, her words echoing in the void:

I didn't do anything to die for. . . . I didn't do anything. . . .

Analyzing Point of View

"The Cold Equations" is told from the **third-person-limited point of view.** This means that the narrator stands outside the action. Answer the questions about the narrator and the point of view in the chart below.

1. Who is the narrator?	
2. What does the narrator know that no one else could know?	
3. What does the narrator *not* know?	
4. How does the point of view affect the way you feel about the characters? Does it make you sympathize more with one character than with another?	
5. Choose a different point of view from which the story could be told. How would the story change if this point of view were used?	

Taste—The Final Frontier

Reading Skill: Generating Research Questions

You're setting out to do a research project. What's your first step? Well, you'll need to generate (come up with) some good questions. Good research questions will lead you to specific information about your topic. Here are some tips:

- **Stay focused.** Focus on one part of your topic. Stick to questions about this one part.
- **Stay interested.** Ask questions that you really want to answer.
- **Do what reporters do.** When reporters investigate a story, their questions begin with *who, what, when, where, why,* and *how.* Asking these ***5W-How? questions*** will lead you to specific information.

The chart below shows the main steps you need to take to write a research paper. For now, focus on reading background information and generating research questions.

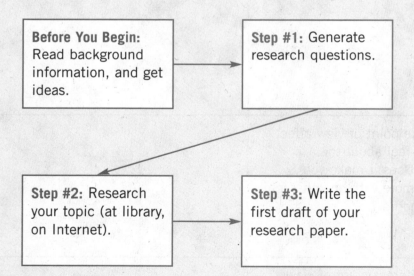

| Before You Begin: Read background information, and get ideas. | → | Step #1: Generate research questions. |

| Step #2: Research your topic (at library, on Internet). | → | Step #3: Write the first draft of your research paper. |

Into the Article

Why don't space travelers like their food? Will future space travelers be able to eat fresh foods grown in space? The following article discusses these questions.

BASED ON THE NEWSPAPER ARTICLE
FROM *The Guardian,* April 21, 2000

Esther Addley

TASTE— The Final Frontier

I think gastronautics seems like an interesting topic for a research paper. Before I do any research, though, I should come up with some good questions. OK, I'll use the *5W-How?* approach: *Why* does space food taste so bad? *What* types of food do astronauts find acceptable? *Who* is Richard Filippi? *Where* is he from? *When* did he create gastronautics? *How* did he create this style of cooking? Now that I have a few questions, I can go to a library to try to find the answers.

Your
TURN

In lines 11–13, we learn that astronauts rely on food to give their days some variety. The daily life of a space traveler could be a topic for your research paper. Write down two research questions about this topic on the lines below:

_____

_____

_____

_____

In 1939, long before the first manned spaceflights, the British interplanetary society suggested fattening up astronauts before and during spaceflights. But because no one knew if humans could swallow in space, Yuri Gagarin, who made the first trip into space,
5 took no food with him.

Since the early 1960s, space food has improved. But today's astronauts agree that it's still pretty awful. The main problem is making space food taste good. In an effort to fix this problem, Richard Filippi invented a cooking style he called "gastronautics" to create
10 food that astronauts might find more acceptable.

Jean Hunter, an associate professor at Cornell University, says a varied diet is important to astronauts. In a place where nothing changes from day to day, food is the most reliable source of variety.

The main complaint is that nothing is fresh. The shuttle may bring
15 fresh fruit. But fruit, even when kept cold, lasts only forty-eight hours in space.

NASA has been looking into growing food in space. Some crops might grow under conditions found on Mars or the moon. Hunter and her group at Cornell developed more than two hundred recipes using
20 plants that could be grown on a moon colony.

To grow in space, plants have to be short. They have to produce well and need little care. Some of the things that could grow well are rice, wheat, potatoes, tomatoes, and several other vegetables. Soybeans would give oil and milk.

25 Because of the limitations for growing food in space, the Cornell group's current recipes are vegan. That is, they use no animal protein.

Hunter says we're a long way from farming animals in space. The first space animal may be carp, a fish that can be grown with very low water use. It will be a long time before astronauts can survive
30 without depending on anything brought from earth. Hunter says, "You might as well bring some food." Tired astronauts might agree. Growing their own food could be too much work. They might settle for a powdered steak sandwich after all.

From "Taste—The Final Frontier" by Esther Addley adapted from *The Guardian*, April 21, 2000. Copyright © 2000 by **Guardian Newspapers Limited.** Retold by Holt, Rinehart and Winston. Reproduced by permission of the publisher.

Research Question Chart

The article you just read provides some good background information about food in space. You can use this information to come up with some questions for a focused research topic. Below is a list of facts from the article. In the column at the right, write at least one question about each fact that will be helpful in your own research. One item has been completed for you.

Facts	Research Questions
1. Richard Filippi invented a cooking style he called "gastronautics" to create food that astronauts might find more acceptable.	Who is Richard Filippi? Where is he from? What kinds of food are acceptable to astronauts? 　Why does space food taste so bad? 　How did Richard Filippi come up with gastronautics?
2. Astronauts' most reliable source of variety during space travel is their food.	
3. Plants should be short, high producing, and need little care to grow in space.	
4. The first space animal may be carp, a fish that can grow with very little water.	

Typhoid Fever

Literary Focus: Voice

In literature, **voice** refers to the writer's use of language and overall style. Writers express their voices through their **diction** (the kinds of words they choose), their sentence structure, and the **tone,** or attitude, that they take toward their subjects and characters. In his memoirs, Frank McCourt uses a unique voice to tell his tragic story of growing up poor in Ireland.

Reading Skill: Evaluating Credibility

Credibility is another word for "believability." Some stories are more believable, or credible, than other stories are. To evaluate (or decide) whether a story is credible, ask yourself a simple question as you read: "Does this sound like it might really happen?" Your answer will tell you whether or not you find the story credible.

Into the Story

"Typhoid Fever" is based on an event in Frank McCourt's boyhood. McCourt grew up poor in Ireland in the 1930s and 1940s. He lived in a crowded slum where diseases like the ones in this story, typhoid (TY foyd) fever and diphtheria (dihf THIHR ee uh), were common. People catch typhoid fever by eating food or drinking water that contains the germs that cause the disease. They catch diphtheria by being in contact with people who already have it.

Both diseases are easy to catch, so sick people are kept away from healthy people. In McCourt's Ireland, the sick were kept in "fever hospitals." As in his story, the Catholic Church ran most of those hospitals, and nuns cared for patients.

McCourt caught typhoid fever when he was ten years old. Like other sick people, he was sent to a fever hospital.

Frank McCourt

FROM Angela's Ashes

TYPHOID FEVER

Your
TURN

EVALUATING CREDIBILITY

Does it seem believable that Frank, who is only ten years old, would think that speaking Shakespeare's words aloud was like "having jewels in my mouth" (lines 29–30)? Maybe the writer, who is now an adult, doesn't remember how he *really* felt about Shakespeare. List two reasons why Frank's response to Shakespeare might be considered credible (believable).

_____

_____

_____

_____

One morning a girl's voice from the next room says, "Boy with the typhoid, are you awake?"

"I am."

"What's your name?"

5   "Frank."

"My name is Patricia Madigan. How old are you?"

"Ten."

"Oh." She sounds disappointed.

"But I'll be eleven next month."

10   "Well, that's better than ten. I'll be fourteen in September."

She tells me she is in the Fever Hospital with diphtheria and "something else," nobody knows what.

Soon Sister Rita is lecturing about no talking between rooms and telling us we should be saying the rosary[1] and giving thanks for

15   our recoveries.

She leaves and Patricia whispers, "Give thanks, Francis, and say your rosary." I laugh so hard the stern nurse from County Kerry[2] runs in to see if I'm all right. She scolds me for laughing and says, "No laughing because you'll damage your internal apparatus!"

20   After she plods out, Patricia whispers again in a heavy Kerry accent, "No laughing, Francis, and pray for your internal apparatus."

Mam visits me on Thursdays. She says my father is back at work at Rank's Flour Mills and please God this job will last a while with the war on and the English desperate for flour.

25   Patricia gives Seamus, the man who mops the floors, a short history of England for me. He tries to sing me a song, but the Kerry nurse threatens to report him to Sister Rita.

The book tells about all the kings and queens of England. It includes the first bit of Shakespeare I ever read. I don't know what it

30   means, but it's like having jewels in my mouth when I say the words.

Patricia reads me a verse from "The Highwayman" every day. I can't wait to learn a new verse and find out what's happening to the highwayman and the landlord's red-lipped daughter. I love the poem

---

1. **rosary:** group of prayers that Roman Catholics say while holding a string of beads.
2. **County Kerry:** The nurse's accent is different from that of the children.

Excerpt (retitled "Typhoid Fever") adapted from *Angela's Ashes* by Frank McCourt. Copyright © 1996 by Frank McCourt. Retold by Holt, Rinehart and Winston. Reproduced by permission of **Scribner, an imprint of Simon & Schuster Adult Publishing Group.**

because it's exciting and almost as good as my two lines of
35 Shakespeare.

Patricia's ready to read the last few verses when in comes the
nurse from Kerry shouting at us. "I told ye there was to be no talking
between rooms. Diphtheria is never allowed to talk to typhoid and
visa versa." And she makes Seamus take me upstairs.

40 He whispers, "I'm sorry, Frankie," as he slips the book under
my shirt and lifts me from the bed.

Sister Rita stops us to say I'm a great disappointment to her
and that I'll have plenty of time to reflect on my sins in the big ward
upstairs and I should beg God's forgiveness for my disobedience
45 reciting a pagan English poem about a thief on a horse when I could
have been praying.

There are twenty beds in the ward, all white, all empty. The
nurse tells Seamus to put me at the far end of the ward to make
sure I don't talk to anyone, which is very unlikely since there isn't
50 another soul on this whole floor. She tells me this was the fever
ward during the Great Famine[3] long ago. She says, "'Twould break
your heart to think of what the English did to us, no pity at all for the
little children with their mouths all green from trying to eat the grass,
God bless us and save us."

55 The nurse takes my temperature. "'Tis up a bit. Have a good
sleep for yourself now that you're away from the chatter with
Patricia Madigan below who will never know a gray hair."

Nurses and nuns never think you know what they're talking
about. You can't show you understood that Patricia is going to die.
60 You can't show you want to cry over this girl who taught you a lovely
poem which the nun says is bad.

Seamus tells me the nurse is a right ol' witch for running to
Sister Rita and complaining about the poem going between the two
rooms. "Anyway, Frankie, you'll be outa here one of these fine
65 days," he says, "and you can read all the poetry you want though I
don't know about Patricia below, God help us."

He knows about Patricia in two days because she collapsed
and died in the bathroom. There are tears on his cheeks when he

---

3. **Great Famine:** When potato crops failed in 1845–1847, about one million people in Ireland starved to death.

Your TURN

EVALUATING CREDIBILITY

Does the description of the nurse's response in lines 36–39 to Frank and Patricia's conversation seem credible (believable) to you? Why or why not?

_____

_____

_____

Here's HOW

VOCABULARY

Pagan, in line 45, sounds like it means "bad." I looked it up in a dictionary, but it means "not Christian, Muslim, or Jewish." Still, I was on the right track. Sister Rita, a nun, certainly meant that it was "bad" when she said it.

Here's HOW

VOICE

In lines 62–64, Seamus (SHAY muhs) says something funny right after Frank realizes that Patricia is going to die. He tells Frank that Sister Rita was wrong for "complaining about the poem going between the two rooms." McCourt has a unique way of combining serious content with comic relief.

70 says, "She told me she was sorry she had you reciting that poem and getting you shifted from the room, Frankie. She said 'twas all her fault."

"It wasn't, Seamus."

"I know and didn't I tell her that."

Now I'll never know what happened to the highwayman and
75 Bess, the landlord's daughter. Seamus says he'll ask the men in his local pub where there's always someone reciting something and he'll bring it back to me.

I can't sleep because I see people in the other beds all dying and green around their mouths and moaning for soup Protestant
80 soup any soup and I cover my face with the pillow hoping they won't come and stand around the bed howling for bits of my chocolate bar.

I can't have any more visitors. Sister Rita says after my bad behavior with Patricia and that poem I can't have the privilege
85 anymore. She says I'll be going home in a few weeks and I must concentrate on getting better.

I don't want to be in this empty ward with ghosts of children and no Patricia and no highwayman and no red-lipped landlord's daughter.

90 Seamus says a man in his pub knew all the verses of the highwayman poem. Seamus has carried me the poem in his head. He stands in the middle of the ward leaning on his mop and recites how Bess warned the highwayman by shooting herself dead with a redcoat's musket and how the highwayman returns for revenge only
95 to be shot down by the redcoats.

> *Blood-red were his spurs in the golden noon; wine-red was his*
> *velvet coat,*
> *When they shot him down on the highway,*
> *Down like a dog on the highway,*
> *And he lay in his blood on the highway, with a bunch of lace at*
> *his throat.*

100 Seamus wipes his sleeve across his face and sniffles. He says, "'Tis a very sad story and when I said it to my wife she cried all evening. Now if you want to know any more poems, Frankie, tell me and I'll get them from the pub and bring 'em back in my head."

Voice

Voice refers to our sense of the writer who has created the work. Voice is created by a writer's **tone** and **diction,** or choice of words.

In the chart below, state briefly what voice or voices you can find in "Typhoid Fever," and then jot down the words, details, or tone that McCourt uses to achieve this voice:

Voice	Words/Details/Tone
1.	
2.	

The Man in the Water

Literary Focus: The Essay—Thinking on Paper

Essays are thought journeys. Essay writers take a subject and look at it from different angles. The subject of an essay can be anything— from where the stars come from to the clothes dryer's habit of eating socks. An essay can be serious and thoughtful, as in the selection you are about to read. Or it can be comic, as in essays by Dave Barry and James Thurber.

Reading Skill: Summarizing Main Idea

The **main idea** is the most important idea in a piece of writing. Main ideas are sometimes, but not always, stated directly. When a writer doesn't say what the main idea is, it's up to you to figure it out. You can use details in the text to infer, or make an educated guess about, what larger idea the writer is getting at. Listing key words and details as you read can help you find the main idea. When you **summarize** an essay, you state its most important idea in your own words. You should also cite some of the essay's key **supporting details.**

Into the Essay

The disaster described in this essay happened on Wednesday, January 13, 1982. It was late afternoon, and Washington, D.C., was covered in wet snow flurries. Just after Air Florida Flight 90 took off from the Washington airport, the plane hit the Fourteenth Street Bridge. It was rush hour. The plane crushed five cars, tipped over a truck, and then plunged into the Potomac (puh TOH muhk) River. Seventy-eight people died, including four motorists. There were only five survivors. The cause of the accident was probably ice on the plane's wings.

BASED ON THE ESSAY BY
Roger Rosenblatt

The Man in the Water

Here's HOW

ESSAY

After reading lines 1–5, I think this essay is going to focus on Roger Rosenblatt's thoughts about an airplane crash. When he says that there was "nothing very special" about this disaster (lines 3–4), I think he means the opposite—there was something that he wanted to write about. That is his "angle."

Here's HOW

SUMMARIZING MAIN IDEA

The key details that may help me figure out the main idea of this essay are in the first two paragraphs. The first detail is the airplane crashing into the bridge. The second detail is the story of the heroes.

Your TURN

ESSAY

After reading this essay, what kind of behavior does the author think is possible for all of us? Do you agree? Why or why not?

_____

_____

_____

_____

_____

As disasters go, this one was not the worst. The airplane hitting a bridge at rush hour was unusual, and it happened in Washington, a city that expects the routine and the ordinary. Still, there was nothing very special in what happened, except death. So why was the shock

5 so great?

Maybe it was because, last Wednesday, the weather met human character, and while ice brought down Flight 90, four heroes showed us the best of human character.

Three of the four heroes can explain why they did what they did.

10 Two members of a park-police helicopter[1] team that risked their lives picking up survivors said that it was in the line of duty. A young man who jumped into the water to drag an injured woman to shore said, "Somebody had to go into the water." No one had to go into the freezing water, but he did.

15 However, it was "the man in the water" who caught our emotions. He was clinging with five others to the tail section of the plane. Every time rescuers lowered a lifeline, he passed it on to another passenger. When the helicopter came back for him, the man had drowned.

Whatever made these men face death to save their fellows does

20 not belong only to them. Everyone feels the possibility. If the man in the water gave a lifeline to the people struggling to survive, he also gave a lifeline to those who watched him.

The odd thing is that we do not really believe the man in the water lost his fight with nature—with the freezing waters of the

25 Potomac. He could not make ice storms, but he could hand life over to a stranger, and that is a power of nature too. The man in the water fought an enemy he could not overcome, and he held it to a standoff.[2] He was the best we humans can do.

---

1. **helicopter** (HEHL uh KOP tuhr).
2. **standoff:** act of facing something and keeping it away.

"The Man in the Water" by Roger Rosenblatt adapted from *Time*, January 26, 1982. Copyright © 1982 by **Time Inc.** Retold by Holt, Rinehart and Winston. Reproduced by permission of the publisher.

Summarizing Main Idea

The **main idea** is the most important idea in a piece of writing. It contains the author's message to the reader.

The center circle below shows the main idea of the essay. In each of the outside circles, list one detail or key word that supports the main idea. One has been done for you.

A young man jumped into the water and saved an injured woman. He said, "Somebody had to go into the water," to save her. He didn't have to save her, but he did it anyway.

Main Idea

Facing death to save someone else is the bravest thing we can do.

If Decency Doesn't, Law Should Make Us Samaritans / Good Samaritans U.S.A. Are Afraid to Act

Reading Skill: Evaluating Arguments

It's hard to get through a day without someone trying to persuade you, usually through an **argument,** a series of statements designed to convince you of something. How can you evaluate all these arguments? The following questions will help you evaluate the **credibility,** or believability, of an author's argument:

1. **What's the claim, or opinion?** The author's **claim** (also called an **opinion**) is often stated in the form of a **generalization** (a broad statement that covers many situations). For example, this is a generalization that states an opinion: *Every eligible citizen should be required to vote.*

2. **What's the support?** Here are some common ways in which authors support their views:

   Logical appeals. Logical appeals include convincing reasons (statements that explain *why* the author holds an opinion) and evidence (specific information that is used to back up a reason).

   Emotional appeals. These appeals stir feelings such as happiness or anger in readers. Emotional appeals are usually accomplished through the use of **loaded words** (words with strong emotional associations) and **anecdotes** (or personal accounts of an event).

3. **Is the evidence comprehensive?** An author must provide sufficient evidence to back up generalizations and to make an argument convincing.

4. **What's the author's intent?** Does the author hold a biased view, or is the author trying to present a reasoned argument?

Into the Articles

The heroes in "The Man in the Water" are examples of people who helped others in an extremely dangerous situation. The following two articles discuss whether such help should be required by law.

If Decency Doesn't, Law Should Make Us Samaritans

BASED ON THE *HOUSTON CHRONICLE* OP-ED PIECE BY

Gloria Allred and Lisa Bloom

Good Samaritans U.S.A. Are Afraid to Act

BASED ON THE *VIRGINIAN-PILOT* EDITORIAL BY

Ann Sjoerdsma

Your
TURN

_____

_____

_____

_____

If Decency Doesn't, Law Should Make Us Samaritans

Witnesses say photographers stood by and snapped pictures while Princess Diana and her companions were bleeding, injured, and dying, rather than aiding them. These accusations have shocked the world.

5   The photographers may be charged with breaking France's law requiring people to help others in distress. Yet in the United States there is no such law. If the accident had occurred here, they could not have been charged with any crime.

If any good is to come of this tragedy, it should be a call to
10 change U.S. law. The law should require each of us to give aid, where possible, to those at risk of serious injury or death.

For example, it is not too much to ask that we call the police or an ambulance when we come upon a major car accident with severely injured people. A few minutes' delay can be the difference between
15 life and death.

Why do so many people ignore the needs of accident and crime victims? Some say they fear that getting involved will take too much time or that they will be hurt themselves. Others say they aren't sure what to do. True, the untrained should not try to give medical aid.
20 However, it takes so little time and effort to phone for help.

The real reason people don't reach out is because they feel disconnected from strangers in need. Yet the child at risk, the injured motorist, the choking restaurant customer could be any one of us or our loved ones. If each of us felt a responsibility to come to the aid of
25 others, we would have a stronger and safer community.

From "If decency doesn't, law should make us samaritans" by Gloria Allred and Lisa Bloom, adapted from *Houston Chronicle*, September 18, 1997. Copyright © 1997 by Gloria Allred and Lisa Bloom. Retold by Holt, Rinehart and Winston. Reproduced by permission of **Gloria Allred and Lisa Bloom.**

Good Samaritans U.S.A. Are Afraid to Act

In Paris, as we've learned since Princess Diana's fatal crash, passersby are required by law to aid victims of accidents. To be "Good Samaritans."

In the U.S.A., passersby can look the other way. We have no legal
5 duty to help.

Now, states such as Minnesota and Wisconsin are passing new laws. These laws require us to help in emergencies, as long as we don't put ourselves at risk.

I'd like to encourage compassion and community. But the Good
10 Samaritan in the Bible didn't have to worry about being sued. Today's Good Samaritan U.S.A. does.

In general, if a Good Samaritan does what a "reasonable person" would do, he won't be held liable for any harm he may cause. But not always.

15 North Carolina law shields "any person who renders first aid or emergency assistance" at a motor-vehicle accident. That is, unless the person's actions amount to "[careless] conduct or intentional wrongdoing."

It may seem unlikely that Good Samaritans would act wantonly.
20 Still, the term is subject to a lawyer's spin. And what exactly are the limits of "first aid" and "emergency assistance"?

Virginia law protects "any person who, in good faith, renders emergency care or assistance, without compensation" to injured people at an accident, fire, or other "life-threatening emergency."

25 Does this law protect doctors?

"Good Samaritans U.S.A. Are Afraid to Act" by Ann Sjoerdsma, adapted from *The Virginian-Pilot*, September 15, 1997. Copyright © 1997 by **The Virginian-Pilot.** Retold by Holt, Rinehart and Winston. Reproduced by permission of the publisher.

Your TURN

EVALUATING ARGUMENTS

What reasons does the writer give to support her opinion that people should not be required by law to be good Samaritans?

_____

_____

_____

_____

EVALUATING ARGUMENTS

What claim does the writer express in lines 29–31?

_____

_____

_____

Physicians without "a duty to treat" (based on an existing doctor-patient relationship) rarely get sued for their emergency treatment. But lawyers can be creative about arguing that such a duty has come up.

I wish we could do as the French do. But our citizens are much
30 too quick to take each other to court. For Americans, moral duty, not legal duty, remains the best guide to emergency aid.

Evaluating Arguments

Analyze the articles you've just read by completing the outlines below.
After you've mapped the writers' arguments, evaluate how **credible,** or
convincing, you find the arguments. Point out any flaws you see in
them.

"If Decency Doesn't . . ." **Writers' Opinion, or Claim:**	
Main Idea:	
Supporting evidence (facts, statistics, etc.)	
Emotional appeals (loaded words, anecdotes, etc.)	
Intent (change thinking or call to action)	
Tone (formal, informal, humorous, etc.)	
"Good Samaritans U.S.A. . . ." **Writer's Opinion, or Claim:**	
Main Idea:	
Supporting evidence (facts, statistics, etc.)	
Emotional appeals (loaded words, anecdotes, etc.)	
Intent (change thinking or call to action)	
Tone (formal, informal, humorous, etc.)	

R.M.S. Titanic

Literary Focus: Irony

Irony is the difference between expectations and reality. In **situational irony,** what happens is the opposite of what you expected to happen or what should have happened. A good example is the sinking of the *Titanic,* which was supposed to be unsinkable. In **dramatic irony,** the reader knows something important that the characters don't know. We, as readers, know that the *Titanic* sank long ago, but the characters in this article do not know that.

Reading Skill: Understanding Text Structures

In this article about the sinking of the *Titanic,* the author has used two kinds of **text structures** to help you keep track of events.

The Roman numbers divide the article into sections.

The time helps you see how quickly events followed one another.

> **I**
> The *Titanic,* the largest. . . .
> **II**
> 12:25 A.M. The *Titanic's.* . . .
> 12:30 A.M. The word is. . . .
> 12:45 A.M. Lifeboats are lowered, but at first, women. . . .
> 1:00 A.M. Slowly the water. . . .

Keeping track of text structures helps you organize your thinking.

Into the Historical Narrative

Where did the name *Titanic* come from? In Greek mythology the Titans are ancient gods who were incredibly strong giants. For a long time they were the supreme rulers of the universe. Perhaps those who named the ship *Titanic* did not know that even the legendary Titans did not rule forever.

Hanson W. Baldwin

R.M.S. TITANIC

I

The *Titanic*, the largest ship ever, began her maiden[1] voyage on Wednesday, April 10, 1912. She was not only the largest ship afloat, but was believed to be the safest, even unsinkable.

5 At 9:00 A.M. Sunday, a wireless[2] message from the *Caronia* warned the *Titanic* of an ice field in her path. At least five wireless ice warnings reached the ship that day. The *Titanic* did not slow down.

At 11:30 P.M. in the crow's-nest,[3] lookout Frederick Fleet gazed down at the dark, silent, cold water. He searched the darkness for 10 the dreaded ice, but saw only stars and sea.

A wire[4] from the *Californian* warned that it was stuck in pack ice.[5] The *Titanic* commanded the *Californian* to stay off the air.

II

Then, about 11:40 . . . a vast, dim, white, monstrous shape rose 15 directly in the *Titanic*'s path. Frantically, Fleet struck three bells[6]—meaning something was straight ahead. He telephoned the bridge.[7]

"Iceberg! Right ahead!"

The first officer ordered a turn. The bow[8] swung slowly left. The 20 monster was almost upon them.

First Officer Murdoch leaped to the engine-room telegraph.[9] Bells clanged. In the engine room the indicators swung to "Stop!" Frantically, the engineers turned great valve[10] wheels and answered the bells . . . There was a slight shock, a brief scraping, a small 25 tilting left. Slabs and chunks of ice fell on the deck. Slowly the *Titanic* stopped.

---

1. **maiden** (MAY duhn): first.
2. **wireless** (WYR lihs): sent by radio waves instead of electric wires.
3. **crow's-nest:** small closed-in platform near the top of a ship's mast.
4. **wire:** telegram.
5. **pack ice:** a large area of floating pieces of ice, frozen together.
6. **three bells:** warning signal.
7. **bridge** (brihj): a raised part of a ship where the captain controls the ship's movements.
8. **bow** (bow): the front part of a ship.
9. **engine-room telegraph** (TEHL uh graf): the apparatus that allows messages to be sent from the engine room to other parts of the ship.
10. **valve:** devices that control the flow of liquids.

Captain Smith hurried to the deck. Murdoch reported the ship had struck an iceberg.

In and around the boiler rooms, men could see that the
30 *Titanic*'s damage was deadly. In ten seconds the iceberg had ripped a three-hundred-foot slash in the ship's bottom.

The call for help went out. Miles away, ships heard it.

The sea surged into the *Titanic*'s hold. At 12:20 the water burst into the seamen's quarters.[11] Pumps strained in the engine rooms,
35 but the water rose steadily.

The lifeboats were prepared. Because there had been no lifeboat drill,[12] many of the crew did not know where to go.

12:25 A.M. The *Titanic*'s position[13] is sent to a fleet of ships: "Come at once. We have struck a berg."
40 12:30 A.M. The word is passed: "Women and children in the boats." Stewards[14] wake the last passengers. The *Carpathia* radios, "Coming hard." The alarm changes the course of many ships—but not of the *Californian*. The operator of the *Californian*, nearby, has put down his earphones and gone to bed.
45 12:45 A.M. Lifeboats are lowered, but at first, women hang back. They hesitate to leave the unsinkable ship for a lifeboat ride on an icy sea. One boat, with room for sixty-five passengers, has only twenty-eight. The band plays ragtime, popular music of the day.
50 1:00 A.M. Slowly the water creeps higher. The "Millionaires' Special" lifeboat, with room for forty, leaves with twelve wealthy passengers while poor immigrants[15] race for space on a boat. The band plays ragtime.

1:20 A.M. Half-filled lifeboats are ordered to take on more
55 passengers, but the boats are never filled. Some boats head for another ship's lights miles away. The lights disappear. The unknown ship steams off. On the *Titanic*, the water rises. The band plays ragtime.

IRONY

Why is the use of the pumps in the engine rooms (lines 34–35) an example of dramatic irony?

_____

_____

_____

_____

UNDERSTANDING TEXT STRUCTURES

How does knowing the exact times (lines 38, 40, 45, 50, and 54) help you realize the danger the ship is in?

_____

_____

_____

_____

---

11. **quarters** (KWAWR tuhrz): the part of the ship where the sailors slept.
12. **drill:** training exercise.
13. **position** (puh ZIHSH uhn): location, where something is.
14. **stewards** (STOO ijrdz): shipboard servants.
15. **immigrants** (IHM uh gruhntz): people who come into a country to live.

60   1:30 A.M. As one boat is lowered into the sea, a boat officer fires his gun to stop a rush of poor people from the lower decks. A woman tries to take her Great Dane on a lifeboat. When she is refused, she steps out of the boat to die with her dog.

     1:40 A.M. Major Butt helps women into the last boats. Colonel John Jacob Astor put his young wife in a boat, saying "I'll join you 65   later." Another woman chooses to stay with her husband.

     2:00 A.M. The *Titanic* is dying now. Her front goes deeper, her back higher. Below, the sweaty firemen[16] keep steam up for the engines.

     660 people are in boats with 1,500 still on the sinking ship.

70   In the radio shack, the operator, sends "SOS—"[17]

     The tired captain appears at the radio-room door. "Men, you have done your full duty. Now, it's every man for himself."

     2:10 A.M. The band plays "Nearer My God to Thee." The water creeps over the bridge where the *Titanic*'s master stands; he steps 75   out to meet it.

     2:17 A.M. The lights flicker out. The engineers have lost their battle.

     2:18 A.M. People leap into the night and are swept into the sea. The *Titanic* stands on end. She slides to her grave—slowly at 80   first, and then faster.

     2:20 A.M. The greatest ship in the world has sunk.

III

The lifeboats pulled safely away from the sinking ship, from the people freezing in the water. Only a few lifeboats were fully loaded. 85   Most half-empty ones did not try to pick anyone up. People on some lifeboats beat away the freezing swimmers.

     Only a few lifeboats had lights. Only No. 2 had a light that helped the *Carpathia*, coming to the rescue. Other ships were rushing to help too, but not the *Californian*.

---

16. **firemen:** men who tended the fires that heated the boilers in the ship. The boilers made steam, which drove the ship's engine.

17. **SOS:** a call for help in code.

90　　At 2:40 the *Carpathia* sighted boat lights. At 4:10 she picked up the first boat and learned that the *Titanic* had sunk. About that time, the *Californian*'s radio operator put on his earphones and learned of the disaster.

IV

95　**O**n Thursday night, when the *Carpathia* reached New York, thirty thousand people jammed the streets as the first survivor[18] stepped down the gangway.

　　Thus ended the maiden voyage of the *Titanic*.

V

100　**E**ventually, people learned the *Titanic* had carried lifeboats for only one third of her load. The boats had been only partly full. Boat crews had been slow in reaching their stations. Warnings of ice ahead had reached the *Titanic*. Her speed was excessive.[19] The posted lookout was inadequate.[20]

105　The *Carpathia* was highly praised; the *Californian* was not. Reports showed that she was probably five to ten miles away from the sinking *Titanic*. She had seen the lights and the rockets. She had not received the wires because her radio operator was asleep.

　　A report stated, "When she first saw the rockets,[21] the

110　*Californian* could have pushed through the ice to the open water easily and so helped the *Titanic*. Had she done so she might have saved many if not all of the lives that were lost."

　　"She made no attempt."

Your TURN

IRONY

What kind of irony is in line 98? Explain your answer.

_____

_____

_____

_____

Your TURN

VOCABULARY

The word *posted* in line 104 can mean "put on duty," "put up notices," or "mailed." Underline the meaning you think it has here. Explain your answer on the lines below.

_____

_____

_____

_____

---

18. **survivor** (suhr VY vuhr): someone who stays alive.
19. **excessive** (ehk SEHS ihv): too great.
20. **inadequate** (ihn AD uh kwiht): not enough.
21. **rockets**: flare shot up in the air as a signal of distress.

Dramatic and Situational Irony

In **dramatic irony** the reader knows something important that the characters don't know. In **situational irony** what happens is the opposite of what is expected to happen or what should have happened.

In the chart below, some incidents from the article are given. On the line before the example, put a **D** if the incident is an example of **dramatic irony.** Put an **S** if the incident is an example of **situational irony.** Then, on the lines below the example, explain your answer. One has been done for you.

_____ 1. A wire from the *Californian* warned that it was stuck in pack ice. The *Titanic* commanded the *Californian* to stay off the air.

_____

_____

_____

_____ 2. The band plays ragtime.

_____

_____

_____ 3. The lifeboats were launched half empty.

_____

_____

_____

__S__ 4. Some boats head for another ship's lights miles away. The lights disappear.

I would expect the other ship to be coming to the rescue of the people in the lifeboats.

But the ship just sails away.

_____

Vocabulary Development

Words with More than One Meaning

Below are words from the selection "R.M.S. Titanic" that have more than one meaning. In the left-hand side of the chart are the words from the selection. In the right-hand side are meanings of each word. Draw a line under the meaning the word has in the selection. The first one has been done for you.

Word	Meanings of the word
1. maiden	<u>first</u> young woman
2. wire	finish line message sent by radio metal thread
3. bow	bend forward politely front part of a ship device for shooting arrows
4. drill	training exercise device for boring holes

Into Thin Air

Reading Skill: Cause and Effect

A **cause** is why something happens; an **effect** is the result of some event. In this selection you will be asked to look for the causes that led to the disaster on Mount Everest. You will also need to look for the effects of certain decisions made by the climbers.

Here is an example of how specific causes lead to a specific effect:

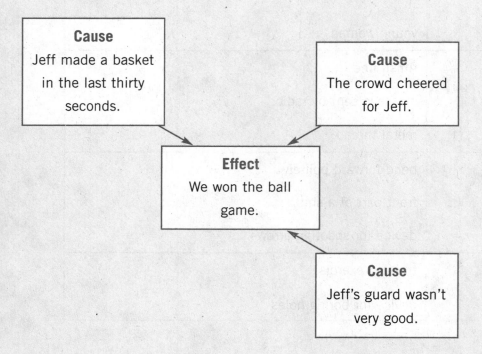

Cause
Jeff made a basket in the last thirty seconds.

Cause
The crowd cheered for Jeff.

Effect
We won the ball game.

Cause
Jeff's guard wasn't very good.

Into the Story

Jon Krakauer, the journalist who wrote this true story, climbed Mount Everest and barely escaped with his life. Krakauer was part of an Everest expedition that ended in the mountain's worst tragedy. The day he reached the summit, ten other climbers died on the mountain. Since the May 1996 tragedy, many more people have paid for a guided climb up the mountain. Some climbers are without experience, and this creates serious dangers.

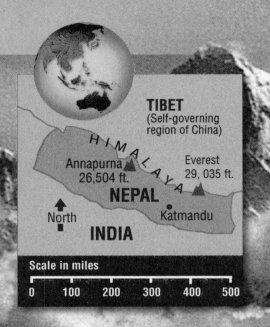

TIBET
(Self-governing
region of China)

HIMALAYA

Annapurna
26,504 ft.

Everest
29, 035 ft.

NEPAL

North

Katmandu

INDIA

Scale in miles

0   100   200   300   400   500

From Into Thin Air

BASED ON THE MAGAZINE
ARTICLE BY

Jon Krakauer

YOU NEED TO KNOW   As Krakauer's account of his climb up Mount Everest opens, he is standing on the top of the mountain. He is in the Death Zone, above 25,000 feet, where the air has so little oxygen that it's almost impossible to breathe. The lack of oxygen makes it difficult for climbers to make sensible and reasonable decisions.

Standing on the top of Mount Everest, I stared dully at the huge curve of earth below. I knew that it was a spectacular sight, but I was too worn-out to care. I had not slept in fifty-seven hours and the oxygen in my tank was low.

5   I took four quick photos of my climbing partners, then started down. After a few steps, I noticed clouds to the south. They looked no different from the harmless puffy clouds that rose from the valley every day.

Later, people would ask why climbers had not paid attention to 10 the warning signs. I saw nothing that afternoon that suggested that a murderous storm was coming swiftly toward us.

After fifteen minutes of very careful shuffling along a seven-thousand-foot drop-off, I arrived at the notorious[1] Hillary Step, named after the first Westerner to climb the mountain. Thirty feet below, 15 three climbers were pulling themselves up the rope, and there were twenty people waiting their turn.

Andy Harris, a guide with my team, came up behind me while I waited to go down. I asked him to turn off the valve[2] on my tank to save oxygen. Not meaning to, Harris opened the valve, and the last of 20 my oxygen was gone. Now I would have to climb down the most unprotected ground on the entire route without oxygen.

Near the end of the group climbing past me were two of my teammates: guide Rob Hall and Yasuko Namba. Doug Hansen—my closest friend while we were on the mountain—also arrived. He 25 mumbled something that I couldn't hear, shook my hand weakly, and continued slowly upward.

---

1. **notorious** (noh TAWR ee uhs): well known because of something bad.
2. **valve** (valv): a device that controls the flow of a gas, such as oxygen.

Adapted from *Into Thin Air* by Jon Krakauer. Copyright © 1997 by Jon Krakauer. Retold by Holt, Rinehart and Winston. Reproduced by permission of **Villard Books, a division of Random House, Inc.**

It was after 2:30 when I made it down to the South Summit. By now the weather did not look so benign.[3] I grabbed a fresh oxygen tank, attached it to my breather,[4] and hurried down into the gathering 30 cloud.

Four hundred feet behind me, where the summit[5] was still in sunlight, my teammates were wasting time taking photos and giving high-fives. None of them suspected that on that day, every minute would count.

35 When I reached the Balcony, about 4 P.M., I found Beck Weathers standing alone, shivering. Due to eye surgery, Weathers could not see at high altitudes. Hall had tried to send Weathers back down, but Weathers talked Hall into waiting to see if his vision[6] improved. If not, Weathers would have to wait at 27,500 feet for Hall and the 40 group to return.

I tried to convince Weathers to come with me, but he decided to wait.

By 5:30, the storm was now a full blizzard.[7] I was only two hundred feet above Camp Four, but I still had to climb down a bulge 45 of rock-hard ice without a rope.

Suddenly, Harris stumbled out of the storm. His cheeks were coated with frost, one eye was frozen shut, and his speech was slurred. He desperately wanted to reach the tents and started scooting down the ice on his butt, facing forward. A second later he lost his 50 grip and went rocketing down on his back.

Two hundred feet below, I could see Harris lying still. I was sure he'd broken at least a leg. Then, he stood up, waved, and stumbled toward camp.

Twenty minutes later I was in my tent, the door zipped tight. I 55 was safe. The others would be coming into camp soon. We'd climbed Mount Everest.

It would be many hours before I learned that everyone did not make it back to camp.

---

3. **benign** (bih NYN): mild; not harmful.
4. **breather** (BREE thuhr): a device for letting air out of a tank.
5. **summit** (SUHM iht): the highest point.
6. **vision** (VIHZH uhn): sense of sight.
7. **blizzard** (BLIHZ uhrd): very cold, snowy storm.

INTO THIN AIR **61**

CAUSE AND EFFECT

Re-read lines 31–34, and draw a line under the sentence that tells you that taking time for photographs on the summit will affect the trip down the mountain.

VOCABULARY

What is a synonym—a word that means the same—for *summit* (line 31; see also "You Need to Know")?

_____

_____

VOCABULARY

The word *vision* in line 38 is defined in a footnote at the bottom of the page. I thought that *vision* could also mean something that I see in my imagination. I looked in a dictionary, and that meaning is also correct.

CAUSE AND EFFECT

Re-read lines 63–68 and then, on the lines below, tell why Hall stayed with Hansen at the top of the Hillary Step.

_____

_____

_____

VOCABULARY

Often a word is defined in the context of the sentence—that is, other words in the sentence tell you the meaning. Re-read lines 79–80, and underline the definition of the word *Sherpas*.

VOCABULARY

I think the word *frostbitten* in line 88 means "frozen." I know that frost is ice. Ice cannot bite, like a dog does, but it could damage and hurt Beck Weathers's hand just as much as a dog bite.

CAUSE AND EFFECT

Beck Weathers had to have his hand amputated (lines 89–90). This operation had to be done because his hand had been frozen.

Hall and Hansen were still on the exposed summit ridge. Hall
60 waited for over an hour for Hansen to reach the summit and return. Soon after they began their descent,[8] Hansen ran out of oxygen and collapsed.[9]

At 4:31 P.M., Hall radioed Base Camp to say that he and Hansen were above the Hillary Step and needed oxygen. Two full bottles were
65 waiting for them at the South Summit, but Harris, in his oxygen-starved confusion, overheard the radio call and broke in to tell Hall that all the bottles at the South Summit were empty. Hall stayed with Hansen at the top of the Hillary Step.

There was no further word from Hall until the middle of the night.
70 He finally reached the South Summit after twelve hours—it should have taken half an hour—but could no longer walk. When asked how Hansen was doing, Hall replied, "Doug is gone."

Late the following day, Hall was connected by radio to his wife in New Zealand. After a few minutes of conversation, Hall told his wife,
75 "I love you. Please don't worry too much," and signed off.

These were the last words anyone heard him say. Twelve days later, Hall was found lying in a shallow ice-hollow, his upper body buried under a drift of snow.

Hutchison and a team of Sherpas, the local guides from Nepal,
80 set out to find the bodies of our teammates Weathers and Namba. Both were found barely alive, covered in thick ice. Hutchison asked Lhakpa Chhiri's advice. Lhakpa Chhiri, a veteran guide respected by everyone for his knowledge of the mountain, urged Hutchison to leave Weathers and Namba where they lay. Trying to rescue them would
85 jeopardize[10] the lives of the other climbers. Hutchison decided that Chhiri was right.

Later that day, Beck Weathers lurched into camp, his horribly frostbitten right hand outstretched in a frozen salute, looking like a mummy in a horror film. A month later, a team of Dallas surgeons
90 would amputate[11] Weathers's dead right hand just below the wrist.

---

8. **descent** (dih SEHNT): a going down; a trip down.
9. **collapsed** (kuh LAPSD): fell down.
10. **jeopardize** (JEHP uhr dyz): put in danger.
11. **amputate** (AM pyuh tayt): to cut off a limb, such as an arm or a leg.

Until I climbed in the Himalayas, I'd never seen death at close range. And there was so much of it: Eleven men and women lost their lives on Everest in May 1996. (After Krakauer wrote this article, a twelfth death was discovered.)

95   Climbing mountains will never be safe. Famous mountain climbers—especially Everest climbers—have always been those who took great risks and got away with it. When given a chance to reach the planet's highest point, people are quick to abandon caution completely. "Eventually," warns Tom Hornbein, thirty-three years

100 after his ascent of Everest, "what happened this season is certain to happen again."

Your TURN

CAUSE AND EFFECT

Why do people keep climbing Mount Everest? Underline the sentence in lines 95–101 that helps answer this question.

Cause-and-Effect Chart

A **cause** is why something happens. An **effect** is the result of some event. One tragic effect of the expedition to climb Mount Everest was the loss of Beck Weathers's right hand. This event is in the Effect box in the center of the graphic organizer. Look back through the story to find as many causes as you can for why this happened, and write them in the Cause boxes. Some have been done for you.

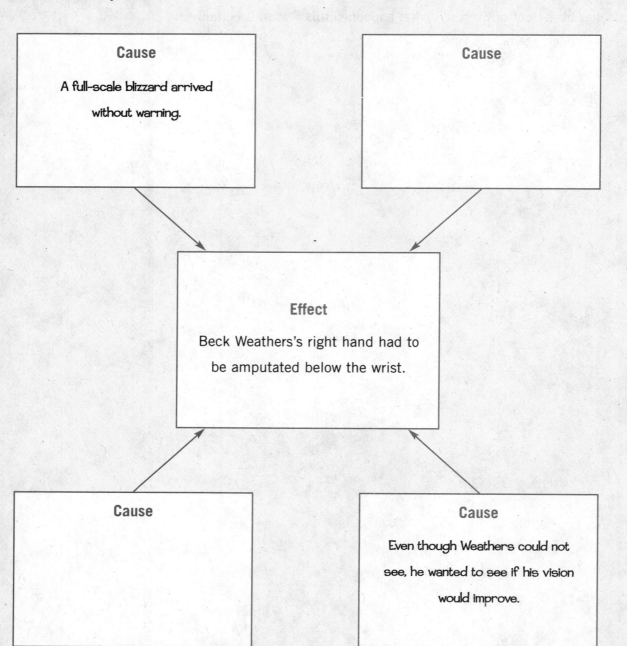

Cause

A full-scale blizzard arrived without warning.

Cause

Effect

Beck Weathers's right hand had to be amputated below the wrist.

Cause

Cause

Even though Weathers could not see, he wanted to see if his vision would improve.

Vocabulary Development

Analogies and Comprehension

A. In an **analogy** the words in one pair relate to each other in the same way that the words in a second pair do. Fill in each blank below with the word from the Word Bank that best completes the analogy. For more help with analogies, see page 7.

see page 7

> **Word Bank**
> summit
> vision
> blizzard
> descent
> collapsed
> amputate

1. BASE : BOTTOM :: _____ : top

2. THUNDERSTORM : RAIN :: _____ : snow

3. HEARING : EARS :: _____ : eyes

4. TRY : ATTEMPT :: _____ : sever

5. CHOSE : PICKED :: _____ : fell

6. DEPARTURE : RETURN :: _____ : ascent

B. Select three words from the Word Bank. Write a sentence for each word.

My word: _____

My sentence: _____

_____

_____

My word: _____

My sentence: _____

_____

_____

My word: _____

My sentence: _____

_____

_____

Vision Quest

Reading Skill: Analyzing an Encyclopedia Article

When you research a topic, a good place to start is with an article in an encyclopedia. To be sure that you get the information you want from the article, ask yourself the following questions:

- Is this article mostly about my research topic? For example, if you want to know all about elephants, you do not want an article that is only about elephants in zoos.
- Is there enough information in this article for my research? If not, you can use terms from the article as the basis for a search in other resources. For example, you could use the term *vision quest* to search in the indexes of books, on the Internet, or in a library catalog.

Into the Article

This article is from the *Encyclopaedia Britannica*. There are many different encyclopedias. Some, such as the *Encyclopaedia Britannica*, cover many different topics. Other encyclopedias focus on a particular subject, such as animals. When you search in an encyclopedia, begin with the index. Sometimes this is a separate book or volume in the set. Other encyclopedias will have an index in each volume.

Vision Quest

BASED ON THE ARTICLE
FROM *Encyclopaedia Britannica, 1995*

Here's
HOW

**ANALYZING AN
ENCYCLOPEDIA ARTICLE**

After reading the first
paragraph (lines 1–9), I know the
main points of the article. 1) Who
goes on the quest. 2) What it is.
3) Tribal differences between
vision quests.

Your
TURN

**ANALYZING AN
ENCYCLOPEDIA ARTICLE**

Re-read lines 5–6 and the
footnote below. What topic
related to the vision quest has
an article in this encyclopedia?

_____

_____

Vision[1] **quest,**[2] among the American Indian hunters of the eastern woodlands and the Great Plains, is a necessary part of a young boy's (or, more rarely, a girl's) initiation[3] into adulthood. The youth was sent out from the camp on a solitary[4] vigil[5] involving fasting[6]

5 and prayer. The purpose of this ritual was to get in touch with his guardian spirit (*q.v.*).[7] The vision quest rituals were different from tribe to tribe. The age at which the quest was to be undertaken, its length and difficulty, and the kind of sign received from the guardian spirit also varied.

10 In some tribes or groups, the youth would watch for an animal that behaved in a meaningful way. In other tribes, he discovered an object (usually a stone), which looked like some animal. In the most usual method of receiving a sign, he had a dream in which his guardian appeared (usually in animal form). This guardian animal

15 gave him instructions, took him on a dream journey, and taught him songs. Upon receiving these signs and visions the youth returned to his home, reported his success, and went to a religious specialist for help in explaining his visions.

The techniques of the vision quest are not confined only to young

20 people just becoming adults. They are the basis for every visionary experience of the Indian. The quest may be that of the ordinary man who wants advice from his guardian. Or it may be the vision quest of the great prophets and shamans who have healing and supernatural powers. Among the South American Indians, only the shaman goes

25 on the vision quest to seek a guardian spirit.

---

1. **vision** (VIHZH uhn): something seen in the imagination, in a dream, or in one's thoughts.
2. **quest** (kwehst): search; journey.
3. **initiation** (ih NIHSH ee AY shuhn): admission into a particular group.
4. **solitary** (SOL uh TEHR ee): alone.
5. **vigil** (VIHJ uhl): staying awake and on watch for some particular purpose.
6. **fasting:** going without food.
7. *q.v.*: abbreviation for Latin *quod vide*, "which see." This abbreviation indicates that the encyclopedia contains a separate entry for "guardian spirit."

Analyzing an Encyclopedia Article

Reading Check

Answer the following questions about the article you just read. One question has been answered for you.

1. What is the main subject of this article?

_____

_____

_____

2. This article tells you that there is an article on a connected topic in the same encyclopedia. How does the article give you this information?

_____

_____

_____

3. Give at least one other topic related to a vision quest that the article tells you about.

_____

_____

_____

4. Name two techniques of the vision quest.

_____

_____

_____

5. Who goes on a vision quest?

Young boys and girls go on vision quests. Adults can also go on vision quests.

In South American tribes, only the shaman goes on a vision quest.

_____

The Masque of the Red Death

Literary Focus: Allegory

An **allegory** is a literary element that writers use when they want
to tell two stories at the same time. One story takes place on the
surface. The other story takes place under the surface where the
story's characters and events stand for abstract ideas, such as
love, freedom, evil, and goodness. On the surface level of pure
storytelling, an allegory must hold our attention. Its characters must
seem believable and interesting enough for us to care about them.
On the allegorical level the ideas in the story must be understood
by us.

Reading Skill: Asking Questions

As you read this story, you'll pause at various points and answer
questions that ask you to sum up what you've read so far. Make
sure you understand the vocabulary (the side notes will help you).
Remember to picture the actions in the story.

Into the Story

The plague that Poe writes about in this story is probably based on
the Black Death that swept Europe and Asia during the fourteenth
century. In less than twenty years it killed as many as two thirds of
the population in some areas. In this story a fourteenth-century
prince gives a costume party, or masque, to try to forget about the
plague raging all around him.

The Masque of the Red Death

BASED ON THE SHORT STORY BY
Edgar Allan Poe

Here's HOW

ASKING QUESTIONS

What is the "Red Death"? It is a horrible disease that causes severe pain, dizziness, and bleeding. It results in death within half an hour.

Here's HOW

ALLEGORY

I know that in allegories, characters often stand for abstract ideas. Prince Prospero could stand for wealth because *Prospero* sounds like *prosperous*, which means "successful and rich."

Your TURN

ASKING QUESTIONS

Describe the seven rooms (lines 15–28) as you picture them.

_____

_____

_____

_____

_____

Here's HOW

VOCABULARY

Usually I think of *struck* as meaning "hit," but in line 29, it seems to relate to the clock. I think in this case *struck* means "announced the hour."

The "Red Death" struck the entire country. No disease had ever been so horrible, or so fatal, as the "Red Death." Its mark was blood—the redness and horror of blood. Sharp pains, sudden dizziness, and bleeding from every pore signaled death within half an hour.

5 But Prince Prospero was happy, brave, and wise. He invited a thousand friends from his court and moved to a remote building. A strong wall and iron gates guarded the building. When everyone was inside, the gates were welded shut to prevent anyone from leaving. There was plenty to eat and drink. With such precautions they could 10 wait out the plague. The world could take care of itself. The prince had provided all kinds of pleasures—clowns, actors, dancers, musicians. Outside, the "Red Death" waited.

After six months, the prince entertained his thousand companions at a masked ball. Let me tell you about the rooms in which it was 15 held. There were seven of them, arranged so no matter where you stood, you could see only one room ahead. On the left and right of each room, in the middle of the wall, a tall and narrow window looked out upon a closed corridor. Each room's walls and furniture were a different color: the first blue, the second purple, the third 20 green, the fourth orange, the fifth white, and the sixth violet. All of these rooms held stained-glass windows of the same color as the room itself. The final room was decorated all in black, with blood-red windows. No lamps or candles burned in any of the rooms. The only light came from a fire held in a brazier, a heater, behind the windows. 25 This light came through the tinted glass. But in the black room, the red light on the black velvet curtains and furniture was so horrible that few dared to go into the room at all.

A huge clock of ebony stood in this room. Its tick was dull and heavy. When it struck the hour, everyone and everything stopped 30 while the deep chimes rang out. The orchestra stopped playing. The dancers paused and grew pale. Each person felt uncomfortable for a moment. When the clock fell silent again, they all would laugh and decide that the clock would bother them no more. But sixty minutes later, it was just the same.

35   In spite of these things, it was a lively and magnificent party. The prince's plans were peculiar, but bold and fiery. He himself directed the arrangement of the seven rooms at this great ball. There was much of the beautiful, much of the wild, much of the bizarre, something of the terrible, and not a little that was disgusting. The

40 dreamlike guests moved about, taking their mood from the rooms, and making the orchestra's wild music seem like the echo of their steps. Then, the ebony clock, standing in the velvet hall, struck and for a moment all was silent except the sound of the clock. But the echoes of the chime died away, and a light, quiet laughter floated

45 after them. But nobody went into the black room; for the night was fading away, and a redder light shone through the blood-colored panes. The blackness of the curtains made the gloom even greater.

    But the other rooms were densely crowded, and the party went on, until at last the clock began to strike midnight. And then the

50 music stopped, as I have told. The dancers were still, and everything uneasily came to an end. But before the sound of the clock's chimes had faded, many in the crowd noticed a new masked figure among them. No one had seen him before. And the rumor of this new presence spread with a buzz of disapproval, of surprise—then, finally,

55 of terror, of horror, and of disgust.

    At such a gathering, no ordinary appearance could have caused such a stir. Almost anything was allowed at this masquerade; but the figure in question had gone beyond even the prince's flexible limits. Even for people to whom life and death are both a joke, there are

60 things which cannot be laughed at. The whole company seemed to feel that the stranger's costume showed neither wit nor good taste. The figure was tall and thin, and shrouded from head to foot. The mask that hid his face looked exactly like that of a crumbling corpse. And yet all this might have been tolerated, if not approved, by the

65 crazy guests. But the figure had gone so far as to assume the *role* of the Red Death. His clothing was dabbled in *blood*—and his face was sprinkled with the scarlet horror.

Your TURN

ASKING QUESTIONS

What effect does the ebony clock have on the partygoers?

_____

_____

_____

_____

Your TURN

VOCABULARY

What clues in line 55 help you to figure out what *terror* means? Explain.

_____

_____

_____

Your TURN

ALLEGORY

Re-read the description of the new guest in lines 62–67. What abstract idea might this figure stand for? Explain.

_____

_____

_____

When the eyes of Prince Prospero fell upon this ghastly image (which slowly and solemnly stalked about among the dancers), he
70 was shaken with a strong shudder either of terror or distaste. But, in the next minute, his face reddened with rage.

"Who dares?" he demanded of those who stood near him—"who dares insult us with this mockery? Grab him and unmask him—that we may know whom we have to hang at sunrise!"
75 The prince stood in the blue chamber as he uttered these words. The words rang throughout the seven rooms loudly and clearly—for the prince was a bold and robust man. At a wave of his hand, the music was turned down. At his side stood a group of pale attendants.

At first, as the prince spoke, there was a slight rushing movement
80 of this group in the direction of the intruder, who slowly walked toward the prince. A certain awe fell over the whole party, and no one would put out a hand to grab the figure. He passed within a yard of the prince, while the crowd drew back from the centers of the rooms to the walls. The figure made his way, with the same solemn stride,
85 through the blue chamber to the purple—through the purple to the green—through the green to the orange—through this again to the white—and even to the violet, before a decided movement had been made to stop him. It was then that Prince Prospero, maddening with rage and the shame of his own cowardice, rushed through the six
90 rooms. No one else followed, because they were all terrified. Prince Prospero carried a drawn dagger and approached to within three or four feet of the retreating figure. Then, the figure turned suddenly and confronted the prince. There was a sharp cry—and the dagger dropped gleaming upon the black carpet, and instantly afterwards,
95 Prince Prospero fell dead. Then, with the wild courage of despair, a group of the guests at once threw themselves into the black room and grabbed the tall figure who stood erect and still in the shadow of the ebony clock. They gasped in horror at finding the wrappings and corpselike mask empty of any body.

100　　And now all knew of the presence of the Red Death, which had come like a thief in the night. One by one in the blood-spattered halls, guests dropped, and they died in the desperate position of how they fell. And the ebony clock stopped as the final guest breathed his last. And the fire went out. And Darkness and Decay and the Red Death
105　held power over all.

ASKING QUESTIONS

Who is the guest? What happens to the partygoers?

_____

_____

_____

_____

Allegory

An **allegory** is a story that combines two stories in one. One takes place on the surface. The other story takes place under the surface, where the story's characters and events stand for abstract ideas or states of being.

In "The Masque of the Red Death," there are several elements in the story that stand for something more than themselves. In the chart below, explain what each of the elements listed might stand for on an allegorical level.

Elements	Allegorical Meanings
1. Prince Prospero	
2. the seven rooms	
3. the clock	
4. the uninvited guest	

Vocabulary Development

Context Clues

The **context,** the words and sentences that surround an unfamiliar word, may provide hints to its meaning. There are different kinds of context clues: **definition, restatement, synonym,** and **antonym.** The following sentences about "The Masque of the Red Death" contain context clues that will help you figure out the meaning of the underlined words. The context clues appear in *italic* type.

SYNONYM

The seventh room brought a ghastly look to the <u>countenance</u>, or *face*, of all who entered it.

ANTONYM

Everyone at the ball viewed the masked stranger *not with approval* but with <u>disapprobation</u>.

Strategies for Using Context Clues

- Think of an unfamiliar word as a blank that needs filling in.

- Re-read the whole sentence, looking for context clues. Nothing in the sentence? Go back a couple of more sentences and forward one or two.

- Try a few synonyms (or definitions), and see if they make sense.

List the context clues that help you guess the meaning of each underlined word in these sentences from the story. Write what you think each word means, and then check a dictionary.

1. "A huge clock of ebony stood in this room. Its tick was dull and heavy. When it <u>struck</u> the hour, everyone and everything stopped while the deep chimes rang out."

2. "And the rumor of this new presence spread with a buzz of disapproval, of surprise— then, finally, of <u>terror</u>, of horror, and of disgust."

3. "When the eyes of Prince Prospero fell upon this ghastly image (which slowly and <u>solemnly</u> stalked about among the dancers), he was shaken with a strong shudder either of terror or distaste."

Shall I Compare Thee to a Summer's Day?

Literary Focus: The Sonnet

William Shakespeare wrote 154 sonnets in all. All Shakespearean sonnets have a set form. The sonnet begins with three four-line units called **quatrains.** The sonnet always ends with two lines, called a **couplet.** Each quatrain makes a point or gives an example. The final couplet sums it all up.

Reading Skill: Finding the Main Idea

Although this sonnet has only fourteen lines, it is packed with ideas and images. As you read, note the ideas or images that seem most important to you. These will often contain the main idea of the poem.

You are lovelier than a mild summer's day.

Main Idea
In my love poem you will live forever.

You will always be lovely.

Into the Sonnet

William Shakespeare had already written many famous plays when his sonnets were published in 1609—apparently without his permission. No one knows when he wrote the sonnets or if the speakers in the poems are real people, imagined characters, or Shakespeare himself.

Shall I Compare Thee to a Summer's Day?

William Shakespeare

In the first line, the speaker starts out by wondering if he or she should compare a loved one to a summer's day. I think the main idea in this sonnet has something to do with love.

Your
TURN

FINDING THE MAIN IDEA

In lines 13 and 14, what does the speaker seem to be saying that this sonnet will do for his or her beloved?

_____

_____

_____

_____

Here's
HOW

VOCABULARY

I looked up *thee* (lines 1 and 14), *thou* (lines 2, 10-12), and *thy* (line 9) in a dictionary. These used to be the "familiar" forms of *you*. I think *familiar* means talking to people you know and love, not strangers. Now everybody is *you*.

YOU NEED TO KNOW   In Shakespeare's day, every gentleman was expected to write sonnets in praise of his loved one. Writing a sonnet was a challenge, a kind of game. The speaker of this sonnet expresses passionate feelings within the very strict rules for writing a sonnet—not an easy job. The sonnet is clearly written about a person. However, the sonnet celebrates the fact that the poem itself will ensure that the lover will be remembered forever—or as long as the poem is remembered. Therefore, it also gives the poet an opportunity to brag about his poetry.

Shall I compare thee to a summer's day?
Thou art more lovely and more temperate.[1]
Rough winds do shake the darling buds of May,
And summer's lease[2] hath all too short a date.
5   Sometime too hot the eye of heaven shines,
And often is his gold complexion dimmed;
And every fair from fair sometime declines,
By chance, or nature's changing course, untrimmed;[3]
But thy eternal summer shall not fade,
10   Nor lose possession of that fair thou ow'st,[4]
Nor shall Death brag[5] thou wand'rest in his shade,
When in eternal lines to time thou grow'st:
    So long as men can breathe or eyes can see,
    So long lives this, and this gives life to thee.

---

1. **temperate** (TEHM puhr iht): mild; constant; well balanced.
2. **lease** (lees): a fixed period of time.
3. **untrimmed:** without trimmings (decorations).
4. **thou ow'st:** you own.
5. **brag:** to boast.

Sonnet

All Shakespearean **sonnets** have a set form and must be written in a certain way. A sonnet always begins with three four-line sections called **quatrains.** Each of these quatrains makes a point or gives an example. A sonnet always ends with two lines called a **couplet.** This is where the speaker sums up all that has been said in the sonnet, giving the reader the main idea.

Use the chart below to show the thoughts in each part of Shakespeare's "Shall I Compare Thee to a Summer's Day?" One part of the chart has been filled in for you.

1. Quatrain 1 (lines 1–4)	**Example or Main Point**
2. Quatrain 2 (lines 5–8)	**Example or Main Point** Nature isn't perfect. Beauty fades away in time.
3. Quatrain 3 (lines 9–12)	**Example or Main Point**
4. Couplet (lines 13–14)	**Main Idea**

Night Calls

Literary Focus: Mood

One of the important elements of fiction is mood. **Mood** is the feeling or atmosphere evoked by a piece of writing. Mood is created by language. Lisa Fugard, who wrote the story you're about to read, creates a powerful mood with her vivid descriptions and **sensory images** of a South African wildlife sanctuary. Her **figures of speech,** or unusual comparisons, also help create the mood.

Reading Skill: Monitoring Your Reading

As you read this story, stop from time to time to think about what you have just read. Consider what is revealed about the characters. Think about the **mood** created by the setting. Notice the writer's use of language, especially her **figures of speech.**

Into the Story

When we love someone, we often try to make our loved one happy by keeping bad news from him or her. Think of how children, in particular, can be affected by the loss of a parent and the grief of a survivor (as in this story). What will those children do to help their parent feel happy again?

Night Calls

BASED ON THE SHORT STORY BY

Lisa Fugard

Here's HOW

MONITORING YOUR READING

I can tell that the narrator feels uncomfortable around her father based on the fact that she moves away from him in the truck (lines 9–11). It seems as if the father also feels uncomfortable around the narrator since he shakes her hand instead of hugging her (lines 5–7).

Here's HOW

VOCABULARY

Based on the context, I can tell that *mimicked* (line 14) has something to do with attracting the birds. It seems as if the narrator must have copied the birds' sounds so well that they moved toward her.

Your TURN

MOOD

In lines 28–31, which images create a mood of sadness and a sense of decay?

_____

_____

_____

_____

My father had very large hands. Once, when I came home from boarding school for the September holidays, he met me at the Modder River train station. I watched him get out of his truck and walk toward me in the dust. He wasn't smiling. As I opened my arms to

5 hug him, I could feel that I was about to cry. Instead of hugging me, though, my father stopped and shook hands with me. My small hands disappeared into his.

In the truck, I wasn't sure how close to him I should sit, so I settled in the middle of my half of the seat. The smell of tobacco,

10 sweat, and brandy overwhelmed me, so I moved closer to the window.

When we arrived at the wildlife sanctuary where my father lived, I got out to open the gate, startling several birds in the process. I mimicked their startled cries so accurately that they began to move

15 toward me. I thought my father would smile at what I had done. When I turned to look at him, though, all I could see was the bright reflection of the sky on the truck's windshield.

At boarding school, I had made myself popular by mimicking bird and animal sounds. I could do it well enough to frighten the younger

20 students. When I came home on a visit, I offered to entertain my father with my calls, but he wasn't interested. After all, he had the real animal sounds all around him.

Now, as my father drove toward our house, I noticed how shabby the animal preserve had become—even the pond my father had dug

25 for my mother years ago, before I was born. My mother had planted it with a variety of water plants, and even during two years of bad drought, my father had kept the pond full of water. Birds flocked to it during this dry spell; my mother counted 107 species in all. Now the pond was stagnant and covered with scum. It made me think of a

30 lonely letter my father had written to me several months ago. I had read it once, and then—frightened—had hidden it away.

I forgot about this strange sadness, though, as my dogs followed me into the house and into my bedroom. There, I examined a photograph of my mother, laughing, at thirty-two. I tried to look at

35 her picture closely, but the dogs would not let me. I ran outside with

"Night Calls" by Lisa Fugard adapted from *Outside*, vol. XX, no. 5, May 1995. Copyright © 1995 by Lisa Fugard. Retold by Holt, Rinehart and Winston. Reproduced by permission of the author.

them, back and forth outside my father's window, shouting with joy. I stopped when I was out of breath, looking at a fenced space beneath a blue gum tree. My father kept a red-crested night heron there, one of the last of its kind.

40   The heron had arrived at the game preserve shortly after my mother's death, when I was eight. After the wreck, my aunt Annette insisted that I could not stay in such a remote place. My mother had tutored me, and with her gone, my father would need to move to where I could go to school and he could get away from his memories.

45 He was just about to resign as warden of the preserve when some park officials brought the red-crested night heron to him, hoping they would find a mate for it nearby. When they released the heron into its cage, the bird went wild trying to escape. When it finally collapsed in exhaustion, my father soothed it and then untied the strip of cloth

50 around the bird's dangerous beak. After this encounter, my father decided to stay on at the nature preserve and to send me to boarding school.

For a while, the heron was in the news, and when I came home from school, my father showed me the latest articles about the bird.

55 Once he even gave me one of its feathers. After two or three years, though, the news died down. There seemed little hope that a mate would be found for the heron, and visitors to the preserve returned to a trickle.

I stared at the pen now and thought about the heron, a large gray

60 bird with a red crest that it raised during the mating ritual. I had never seen the crest, and I didn't need to look at the bird now. I climbed the blue gum tree anyway and watched from above as the heron pecked without interest at his food. I had done this many times before, watching my father feed the bird, collect the feathers it lost,

65 and show it off to visitors.

The day was over and it was getting cold. Walking along the outside of the house, I looked into the rooms we had quit using when my mother died. In the living room, her desk was still piled with her books. Inside, I found my father in the kitchen, heating canned food

VOCABULARY

What context clues in lines 42–44 help you to figure out the meaning of *remote* in line 42? Explain.

_____

_____

_____

MONITORING YOUR READING

What event persuades the narrator's father to stay on at the preserve?

_____

_____

_____

MOOD

The details about the heron (its lack of a mate, disinterest in its food, its sad call) all seem to add to the lonely mood of the story.

VOCABULARY

What hint in line 71 indicates the meaning of *frolicking* in that line? Explain.

_____

_____

_____

MONITORING YOUR READING

Re-read lines 80–86. What does the narrator's father do with the heron?

_____

_____

_____

MONITORING YOUR READING

What details in lines 87–102 reveal the father's attitude toward the heron?

_____

_____

_____

70 for dinner. We ate quietly. Afterwards, I felt awkward alone with my father. I missed frolicking with my dogs and running around outside.

At ten o'clock, my father went to bed. In bed myself, I listened to the sounds of animals calling in the darkness. Then I heard the gate creak on the heron's pen. I got up and felt my way through the house
75 and to the window of my parents' old bedroom. From there, I could see my father gently carrying the beautiful, sharp-beaked bird in the moonlight. My father slipped out with the heron, and I went back to bed. Later I heard the heron's sad, trembling call, and I thought of my father and the bird, down by the river in the dark.

80 The next morning, my father covered for the bird's disappearance by suggesting that a hyena had broken into the pen. There was even a hole in the fence to go with his story. My father's mood seemed lighter than the day before. He chatted with me about school, and that night we shared fried bananas and ice cream. Just before
85 bedtime, I looked in the mirror and noticed that I have my father's eyes.

Shortly after we went to bed, I heard the heron's call. I knew that my father heard it too, and I wondered if hearing it made his heart pound the way mine did. I thought of the bird as the last of its kind,
90 and I pictured it stepping delicately in the river water, its red crest raised.

The next night when the heron called, I heard my father's footsteps too. For ten nights, he left the house to follow the heron's call. During the days, we cleaned up my mother's pond and collected
95 water lilies from the river for it. On the drive back with the lilies, I looked for the heron. We even repaired one of the park's trails.

Then one night, the heron didn't call, and the next morning my father's eyes looked lifeless and sad. Afterwards, he was restless for days. He was always walking off somewhere and never sat still for
100 long when he came back to the house. When I watched him from my perch in the blue gum tree, he always returned to the river and then kept walking until I lost sight of him.

One afternoon, I was out looking for snakeskin for a school biology project. I was searching a rocky area, when I came across the

105 remains of a dead bird. I could tell from the gray color that it was the
red-crested heron. I made a shallow grave for the bird and put a large
rock in place over that.

My father didn't come home from his rambling that night. I
waited until ten o'clock, then walked down to the river and hid
110 myself in the reeds along the bank. An hour later, my father arrived,
clearly looking and listening for the red-crested heron. From my
hiding place, I leaned back and did a perfect imitation of the heron's
sad trembling call. My father stood up and looked toward where I was
hiding. I made the sound again and again. He stepped in my
115 direction, his large hands fluttering as lightly as moths.

Here's HOW

VOCABULARY

It seems as if the word *restless* (line 98) has something to do with not being able to stay still. The next sentence says he goes off walking a lot and has trouble sitting still. I checked in a dictionary and found out that *restless* means "an inability to rest or relax."

Your TURN

MONITORING YOUR READING

What does the narrator do for her father at the end of the story? Why does she do this?

_____

_____

_____

_____

_____

Mood

Mood is the feeling or atmosphere evoked by a piece of writing. Mood is often evoked by descriptions that contain words with powerful emotional overtones. Here are some passages from "Night Calls" that use powerful words. On the lines below each passage, describe briefly what mood the passage suggests to you and why:

1. "As I opened my arms to hug him, I could feel that I was about to cry. Instead of hugging me, though, my father stopped and shook hands with me. My small hands disappeared into his." (lines 4–7)

   _____

   _____

   _____

2. "Now the pond was stagnant and covered with scum. It made me think of a lonely letter my father had written to me several months ago. I had read it once, and then—frightened—had hidden it away." (lines 28–31)

   _____

   _____

   _____

3. "The day was over and it was getting cold. Walking along the outside of the house, I looked into the rooms we had quit using when my mother died. In the living room, her desk was still piled with her books. Inside, I found my father in the kitchen, heating canned food for dinner." (lines 66–70)

   _____

   _____

   _____

4. "From my hiding place, I leaned back and did a perfect imitation of the heron's sad trembling call. My father stood up and looked toward where I was hiding. . . . He stepped in my direction, his large hands fluttering as lightly as moths." (lines 111–115)

   _____

   _____

   _____

Vocabulary Development

Verifying Meanings by Examples

You can own a new word (that is, add it to your working vocabulary) by using it, especially by giving examples of the word in action. Use complete sentences to write your answers to the questions that follow.

1. If someone <u>mimicked</u> your speech, what did he or she do? What other things might someone have <u>mimicked</u>?

_____

_____

_____

2. If you are camping in a <u>remote</u> wilderness, what dangers might you face?

_____

_____

_____

3. If someone is <u>frolicking</u> through a park, what might he or she be doing?

_____

_____

_____

4. Describe two situations that might make a person feel <u>restless</u>.

_____

_____

_____

_____

Call of the Wild—Save Us!

Reading Skill: Evaluating the Author's Argument

Persuasive writing tries to persuade you to believe an idea or take an action. To decide whether a writer's argument is believable and should persuade you, take these steps:

1. **Follow the author's argument.** An **argument** is a series of statements designed to persuade you. Usually it begins with a clear statement of the writer's **opinion** or **claim.** Then, to persuade you, the writer provides **reasons** as well as **evidence** to back up those reasons.

2. **Evaluate the support.** Don't believe anyone who tries to convince you by saying, "Because I say so." Make sure the author's opinions and generalizations are supported with enough evidence to be convincing. Evidence includes **logical appeals,** such as facts, statistics, examples, and expert opinions. **Emotional appeals** can support an argument, but they are not evidence. Be sure to distinguish **facts** (statements that can be proved true) from **opinions** (statements that can't be proved.)

3. **Look at structure.** When you're analyzing a piece of persuasive writing, it's important to identify the writer's **main ideas** and the order in which they are presented. Are the main ideas convincing? Are they presented in a logical order?

4. **Identify the author's intent.** In a persuasive piece the author's **intent** is clearly to persuade you, but of what exactly? Sometimes the writer's goal is just to change your thinking, but often it is a **call to action,** asking you to go out and *do* something.

5. **Identify the author's tone.** Identifying the author's **tone,** or attitude toward the subject or audience, may help you evaluate the credibility of an argument. For example, if the intent is to persuade, the tone might be serious or concerned.

6. **Evaluate the author's credentials.** Before you decide how to respond to the persuasion, evaluate the writer's **credibility.** How knowledgeable is the writer about the subject being discussed? Is the writer an expert? What are his or her qualifications?

Call of the Wild— Save Us!

BASED ON THE ARTICLE
FROM *Good Housekeeping,* April 1991

Dr. Norman Myers

YOU NEED TO KNOW In this article you'll read about how each of us can help save plants and animals from extinction (ehk STIHNGK shuhn). When a plant or animal becomes extinct, all of that kind of plant or animal is no longer living. For example, dinosaurs are extinct. The danger of extinction to many plants and animals is becoming common in our modern world.

A species[1] is a type of plant or animal like none other in the world. Each day we lose roughly 50 to 100 wildlife species. Because we chop down forests, pollute[2] rivers and lakes, and drain marshes, we destroy the places where wildlife species live.

5 We drive thousands of plant and animal species into extinction[3] every year. When a species is gone, it's gone for good.

We Are All Losers

Half of the medicines we need come from wildlife species. The value of all these medicines worldwide is more than $400 million a year. A

10 wild plant provided a big breakthrough against cancer. Doctors believe there could be at least ten forest plants that could be used to make superstar drugs against terrible diseases. But scientists have to get to those plants before the places where they live are destroyed.

It makes sense financially to save wildlife species. But should we

15 not consider another argument, the moral[4] one? What right have we, one species, to knock off[5] other species in vast[6] numbers?

We are the only species that can take the life of another species. Yet we are also the only species that can save other species. The U.N.[7] is putting together an agreement to save wildlife wherever it occurs.

---

1. **species** (SPEE sheez).
2. **pollute** (puh LOOT): make dirty and unhealthy.
3. **extinction** (ehk STIHNGK shuhn): state of no longer living on the earth.
4. **moral** (MAWR uhl): decent; proper.
5. **knock off**: kill.
6. **vast**: huge.
7. **U.N.**: United Nations.

"Call of the Wild—Save Us!" by Norman Myers adapted from *Good Housekeeping*, vol. 212, April 1991. Copyright © 1991 by **Norman Myers.** Retold by Holt, Rinehart and Winston. Reproduced by permission of the author.

What Will It Cost?

20 The cost will probably be billions of dollars a year. Rich nations must pay for activities to save wildlife in poor countries that cannot afford such efforts. There are 1.2 billion of us in the world's rich nations. If the bill were about $2.5 billion a year, we would each pay just over $2 **25** per year. The question is "How can we possibly afford *not* to do it now?"

What We Can Do

We can write checks to groups that work to save wildlife. We can write to our elected representatives to persuade[9] them to support laws **30** that help wildlife. More important, we can figure out how to live in ways that cut back on too much buying and wasting. We need to drive cars that use less gas. We need to do more recycling.[10]

The children of the future will wonder why we didn't do more to tackle the threat to wildlife. If we get our act together, future children **35** will marvel[11] at how we saved millions of wildlife species. We still have time, though not much time. The species out there are waiting to hear from us.

EVALUATING THE AUTHOR'S ARGUMENT

What is the author's central claim? What is his intent?

_____

_____

_____

_____

VOCABULARY

The word *checks* in line 28 can mean "marks," "orders for money," or "examines." Underline the meaning you think it has here. Then, explain your answer.

_____

_____

_____

_____

_____

---

9. **persuade** (puhr SWAYD): to win over.
10. **recycling:** putting things to further use.
11. **marvel:** to wonder.

Evaluating an Author's Argument

Use the chart below to evaluate the author's argument. First, identify the author's purpose, or intent. Then, list the best examples of the four types of support the author uses. Next, describe the tone of the piece. Finally, comment on how successful the author was in convincing you of his opinion. One of the boxes has been filled in for you.

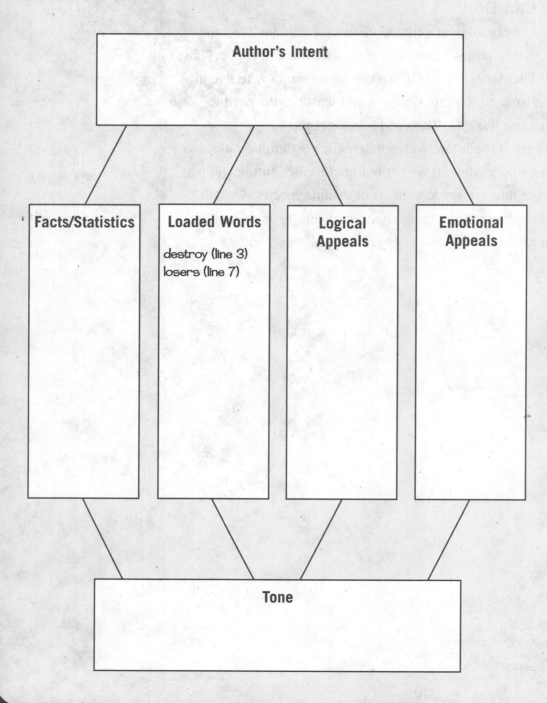

Author's Intent

Facts/Statistics

Loaded Words

destroy (line 3)
losers (line 7)

Logical Appeals

Emotional Appeals

Tone

Vocabulary Development

Using Context Clues

Context clues are words in a sentence that surround a word you
don't know. If you know these surrounding words, they can help you
understand the meaning of the word that you don't know. Use context
clues in the following sentences to help you choose the correct Word
Bank word for each blank. Then, underline the context clues. One has
been done for you.

Word Bank
extinction
species
pollute
moral
vast

1. We _____pollute_____ the water we drink when we allow it to become <u>dirty
   and filled with things that are bad for our health.</u>

2. A plant or animal that is different from all others in the world is a

   _____.

3. There are a _____ number of species in the world, and many are
   becoming extinct.

4. This article is concerned with the growing problem of the _____ of
   many plant and animal species.

5. Doing the right thing is the _____ side of the problem of extinction.

My Sentence

Select one of the words from the Word Bank, and write a sentence of your
own on the lines below. Be sure to include context clues that will help a
reader understand the word you have chosen. Underline these context clues.

_____

_____

_____

_____

Where Have You Gone, Charming Billy?

Literary Focus: Understanding Historical Context

All stories have settings. Most stories also have **historical context**. That
is, they may include details about the events and people of a
particular time. To understand fully the characters and their actions,
you need to know something of that time.

1960s	1970s	1980s	1990s	present
events & people	events & people	events & people	events & people	

Reading Skill: Making Inferences

An **inference** is an educated guess—you make such guesses all the
time. Suppose your friend, who's never late, doesn't appear at the
usual time to pick you up for school. You infer that something's
happened (like a traffic jam) to delay her or maybe she's sick.

Similarly, when you read a story, you fill in missing information
by making guesses about what's left unsaid or unclear.

Into the Story

When Vietnam divided into Communist North Vietnam and non-
Communist South Vietnam, the United States supported the South.
In 1965, President Johnson sent the first U.S. troops to the region.
By 1969, 540,000 American troops were in Vietnam. Ground troops,
like the men in this story, fought to destroy Communist strongholds
in South Vietnam. Often fighting was disorganized, and small groups
of enemy soldiers would attack U.S. troops unexpectedly.

Tim O'Brien, the author of this story, was drafted in 1968 and
spent two years as a soldier in Vietnam.

Where Have You Gone, Charming Billy?

BASED ON THE
STORY BY
**Tim
O'Brien**

Here's
HOW

MAKING INFERENCES

Paul is really worried about being afraid. He keeps telling himself that he won't be afraid once they reach the ocean. He also says that he's afraid of being "so terribly afraid again." I'll bet that this story will be about fear or bravery, but I can't tell yet.

Here's
HOW

VOCABULARY

The word *inert* (ihn URT) in line 26 is new to me. The sentence makes it sound as if *inert* means the opposite of *alert*. I checked in a dictionary, and I was close. *Inert* means "unable to move."

The platoon[1] of twenty-six silent soldiers moved slowly in the dark. One by one they stopped at the rice paddy[2] and squatted quietly in the shadows. At the rear, Private First Class Paul Berlin was pretending he had not watched Billy Boy Watkins die of a heart attack
5 that afternoon.

In the morning, when they reached the sea, PFC Berlin would forget how frightened he had been on his first day at the war. The second day would not be so bad.

A shadow whispered, "We're *moving*. Get up."
10 "Okay," said PFC Berlin.

It was a dark, clear night. Wading through the paddy, he tried not to think. He now knew that fear came in many kinds. In the hot afternoon the fear had been bundled and tight as he crawled like an ant escaping a giant's footsteps, watching Billy Boy Watkins die. Now
15 he feared being so terribly afraid again.

To keep from thinking, he sang songs in his thoughts as he walked toward the sea. *Where have you gone, Billy Boy, Billy Boy, oh, where have you gone, charming Billy? I have gone to seek a wife, she's the joy of my life, but she's a young thing and cannot leave her*
20 *mother.*[3]

When he reached the sea, he would dig a deep hole in the sand and he would sleep and he would not be afraid anymore.

The moon came out, pale and shrunken.

He walked carefully, remembering what he'd been taught. Stay off
25 the center of the path, where the land mines[4] and booby traps were planted. Stay alert. Better alert than inert. He could not remember how to stop being afraid.

Stretching ahead of him, the string of nameless shadow soldiers moved with the slow grace of smoke. Mostly the soldiers were quiet
30 and hidden and seemed far away.

---

1. **platoon:** two or more squads of soldiers under a lieutenant's command.
2. **paddy:** ricefield.
3. The song "Billy Boy" is usually identified as a children's song.
4. **mines:** in this case, explosive devices used to eliminate enemy soldiers or equipment.

"Where Have You Gone, Charming Billy?" slightly adapted from *Going After Cacciato* by Tim O'Brien. Copyright © 1975, 1976, 1977, 1978 by Tim O'Brien. Retold by Holt, Rinehart and Winston. Reproduced by permission of **Dell Publishing, a division of Random House, Inc.**

So he counted his steps. When he had reached 3,485, the column stopped.

One by one the soldiers knelt or squatted down.

PFC Berlin lay back. He might have slept. "I *wasn't* afraid," he was
35 screaming or dreaming, facing his father's stern eyes. When he opened his eyes, a soldier was beside him, chewing a stick of Doublemint gum.[5]

"You sleepin'?" the soldier whispered.

"Hell, no," said PFC Berlin.

40 The soldier took a swallow from his canteen and handed it through the dark. "You're the new guy?"

"Yes." He did not want to admit to being new to the war.

The soldier handed him a stick of gum. "Chew it quiet—OK?"

They chewed the gum until all the sugars were gone; then the
45 soldier said, "Bad day today, buddy."

PFC Berlin nodded but did not speak.

"It's not always so bad," the soldier whispered. "You get used to it."

They were quiet awhile. And the night was quiet, and it was hard
50 to imagine it was truly a war.

"What's your name, buddy?"

"Paul."

"Nice to meet ya. Mine's Toby. Everybody calls me Buffalo, though."

55 The moon was high and bright, and they were waiting for cloud cover. The soldier suddenly snorted. "Can't get over old Billy Boy croaking[6] from a lousy heart attack. . . . Ever hear of such a thing?"

"Not till now," said PFC Berlin.

"Tough as nails . . . . And what happens? A heart attack. Can you
60 imagine it?"

PFC Berlin wanted to laugh. "I can imagine it." He giggled. He imagined Billy's father opening the telegram: SORRY TO INFORM YOU THAT YOUR SON BILLY BOY WAS YESTERDAY SCARED TO DEATH IN ACTION IN THE REPUBLIC OF VIETNAM. . . . Berlin's body shook with giggles.

---

5. **Doublemint gum:** popular brand of chewing gum.
6. **croaking:** here, slang term meaning "dying".

Here's HOW

UNDERSTANDING HISTORICAL CONTEXT

At first, I didn't understand why Paul is told to chew his gum quietly in line 43. Then I remembered that fighting was disorganized and that U.S. troops were attacked unexpectedly. If U.S. troops didn't know where enemy soldiers were, they'd have to be very careful about making noise. Even the sound of gum popping might give their positions away. That would explain why the soldier is worried about the gum.

Your TURN

UNDERSTANDING HISTORICAL CONTEXT

Re-read lines 61–64. Then, draw a circle around the sentence that tells how the U.S. government told relatives of a soldier's death.

VOCABULARY

In line 74–75, Doc Peret "stuck" Billy with the drug morphine. In that sentence, what does "stuck" mean?

_____

_____

_____

Your TURN

MAKING INFERENCES

What change do you think Paul Berlin is undergoing in lines 91–96?

_____

_____

_____

_____

65   The big soldier hissed at him to shut up, but he could not stop giggling and remembering the hot afternoon, and how they'd started on the day's march, and how a little while later poor Billy Boy stepped on the mine, and how it made a tiny little "poof," and how Billy Boy stood there with his mouth wide open, looking down at
70   where his foot had been blown off.

"War's over, Billy," the men had said, but Billy Boy got scared and started crying and said he was about to die. "Nonsense," the medic[7] said, but Billy Boy kept bawling, his face going pale and his veins popping out—scared stiff. Even when Doc Peret stuck him with
75   morphine, Billy Boy kept crying.

"Shut up!" the big soldier hissed, but PFC Berlin could not stop giggling, the same way Billy Boy could not stop bawling that afternoon.

Afterward Doc Peret had explained: "You see, Billy Boy was scared
80   he was gonna die—so scared he had himself a heart attack—and that's what really killed him."

So they wrapped Billy in a plastic poncho,[8] his eyes still wide open and scared stiff, and they carried him over the meadow to a rice paddy. And then the mortar rounds[9] were falling everywhere, and the
85   Medevac[10] helicopter pulled up, and Billy Boy came tumbling out, falling slowly and then faster, and the paddy water sprayed up.

Later they waded in after him, probing for Billy Boy in the stinking paddy, singing—some of them—*Where have you gone, Billy Boy, Billy Boy, oh, where have you gone, charming Billy?*
90   "Shut up!" the soldier said loudly, shaking him.

But PFC Berlin could not stop. The giggles were caught in his throat, drowning him in his own laughter: scared to death like Billy Boy. A fine war story. He would tell his father how Billy Boy had been scared to death, never letting on. . . . He could not stop.
95   The soldier smothered him. PFC Berlin tried to fight back, but he was weak from the giggles.

---

7. **medic:** soldier or sailor trained to provide first aid.
8. **poncho:** waterproof garment with a central slit through which the head can pass.
9. **mortar rounds:** artillery shells fired from short cannons.
10. **Medevac** (MEHD ih VAK): helicopter used to remove wounded soldiers from a combat area.

The moon was under the clouds and the column was moving. The soldier helped him up. "You OK now, buddy?"

"Sure."

100   "You got to stay calm, buddy." The soldier handed him his rifle. "You'll get better at it."

He turned away, and still shivering, PFC Berlin hurried after him.

He would do better once he reached the sea. A funny war story that he would tell to his father, how Billy Boy Watkins was scared to
105 death. A good joke. But even when he smelled salt and heard the sea, he could not stop being afraid.

Your TURN

MAKING INFERENCES

Why do you think Paul Berlin is still very afraid at the end of the story?

_____

_____

_____

_____

Making Inferences

In the chart below, make **inferences,** or educated guesses, about the various parts of the story that are listed. Then, explain what in the story led you to make these inferences.

Event from the Story	Inference	Explanation
1. Paul was "pretending he had not watched Billy Boy Watkins die of a heart attack. . . ." (lines 3–5)		
2. "'It's not always so bad,' the soldier whispered. 'You get used to it.'" (lines 47–48)		
3. "'Shut up!' the big soldier hissed, but PFC Berlin could not stop giggling, the same way Billy Boy could not stop bawling that afternoon." (lines 76–78)		
4. Paul thought: "But even when he smelled salt and heard the sea, he could not stop being afraid." (lines 105–106)		

Vocabulary Development

Question and Answer

Word Bank
inert
paddy
mine
medics
stuck

Each of the following items has a Vocabulary word in italics. Answer the question. Then, explain your answer on the lines provided.

Example: Billy Boy Watkins wound up *croaking* from fright. Does that mean that he was so frightened that he made frog sounds? No.

Explanation: *Croaking* is a slang word for "dying."

1. Paul remembers that it's better to be alert than *inert*. Does that mean that it's better to be alert than scared? _____

   Explanation: _____

   _____

2. When the troops look for Billy Boy's body in the rice *paddy*, are they looking inside a large truck? _____

   Explanation: _____

   _____

3. After seeing Billy Boy get wounded, Paul must have been afraid of stepping on *mines*. Does that mean that he was afraid of stepping into deep holes dug into the earth? _____

   Explanation: _____

   _____

4. Are *medics* trained to give first aid on a battlefield? _____

   Explanation: _____

   _____

5. After Billy Boy had been *stuck* with morphine, he continued to cry. Does that mean that he had been left behind? _____

   Explanation: _____

   _____

The War Escalates / *From* Declaration of Independence from the War in Vietnam

Reading Skill: Balancing Viewpoints

Have you ever noticed that some people stick to facts alone when they talk about a set of events? Their accounts are **objective,** or without personal bias. Other people include only their own feelings and opinions in what they say. Their accounts are heavily **subjective,** or personally biased. Still others give **balanced** accounts. Parts of what they say are **objective,** while other parts are **subjective.**

As you read, pay attention to how well balanced a viewpoint the authors present. Stop now and then to ask yourself these questions: Did a personal bias sneak by me? What was that bias? Did the author use objective information to make a point? What was that information?

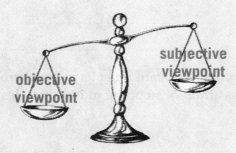

objective viewpoint

subjective viewpoint

Into the Sources

The Vietnam War (1961–1975) was a civil war between non-Communist South Vietnam and Communist North Vietnam. The United States backed South Vietnam. The two excerpts you are about to read will give you information about this war from two different viewpoints. One excerpt is from a chapter in a recent textbook. It has a relatively objective viewpoint. The other excerpt is from a 1967 speech by the civil rights leader Martin Luther King, Jr. It has a relatively subjective viewpoint.

The War Escalates

BASED ON AN EXCERPT FROM The American Nation,

A TEXTBOOK BY Paul Boyer

Declaration of Independence from the War in Vietnam

BASED ON AN EXCERPT FROM THE SPEECH BY
Martin Luther King, Jr.

YOU NEED TO KNOW By 1968, more than 500,000 U.S. troops were in Vietnam, but the antiwar movement was growing at home. By the time U.S. troops left Vietnam in 1973, more than 50,000 U.S. soldiers had died in the war.

The War Escalates

"The enemy has attacked United States ships in the Gulf of Tonkin. These attacks have required me to order the armed forces of our country to take action in reply. The first attack on the destroyer Maddox, on August 2, was repeated today. Several enemy ships
5 *attacked two U.S. destroyers. . . . We believe at least two enemy boats were sunk. There were no U.S. losses. . . .But repeated attacks against the United States must be met not only with alert defense, but with a strong reply. That reply is being given even as I speak. Our planes are now attacking gunboats and support areas in North Vietnam."*
10 —adapted from a nationally televised speech by Lyndon B. Johnson, August 4, 1964

President Johnson's speech that night marked a U.S. buildup in the Vietnam War.

The Tonkin Gulf Resolution

15 In 1963 Secretary of Defense Robert S. McNamara told President Johnson that he needed to increase U.S. military forces in South Vietnam. He said this had to be done to prevent a Communist victory. Johnson had to get backing from Congress before expanding the war. The Gulf of Tonkin events gave Johnson the chance
20 he needed.

Johnson asked Congress to give him the power to use military force "to prevent further aggression." Both houses of Congress passed the **Tonkin Gulf Resolution.** It gave Johnson the power to take "all necessary measures to repel[1] any armed attack" against
25 U.S. forces.

---

1. **repel** (rih PEL): to force away; to fight against.

Johnson claimed that the Communists had attacked first. The truth is, the U.S. destroyer *Maddox* had fired first. The second attack may never have happened. Some U.S. sailors apparently had misread their radar. But Johnson and his advisers got what they wanted: the power to expand the war.

By passing the resolution, Congress gave up its power to declare war. As Senator Wayne Morse pointed out, "We are in effect giving the President war-making powers in the absence of a declaration of war."

U.S. Forces in Vietnam

President Johnson soon called for an escalation, or buildup, of U.S. forces. In April 1965, more than 13,000 young men were drafted to serve in the armed forces.

The troops. More than 2 million Americans served in Vietnam. At first, most were professional soldiers who had enlisted. Later, more draftees were shipped to Vietnam. The average U.S. soldier in Vietnam was younger than those who had served in World War II or the Korean War. He was also poorer and had less education.

Young men from families with higher incomes were least likely to serve in Vietnam. They got deferments, postponements of service, mostly because they were going to college.

African Americans and Hispanics served in combat in very high numbers. In 1965 almost 24 percent of all battle deaths were African American. Yet they made up just 11 percent of the total number of people in the United States.

Soldiers in Vietnam faced terrible hardships. Some faced the enemy in battles. Others cut their way through jungles. They heard but did not see the enemy. Others searched house to house for enemy soldiers. Most Americans served in support jobs. But no one who served in Vietnam was safe. Rockets could strike anywhere.

Some 10,000 servicewomen had noncombat jobs in Vietnam, mostly as nurses. They faced the horrors of war daily. Another 20,000 to 45,000 women worked as civilians for groups such as the Red Cross.

Here's HOW

VOCABULARY

I'm not sure what *escalation* means in line 36. Maybe it's related to *escalator* and means something that moves up? Yeah, that's right. The next word, *buildup*, repeats the meaning of *escalation* in another way. So, an escalation of troops means that the number of soldiers increased, or went up.

Your TURN

VOCABULARY

Circle any words in lines 44–46 that help you understand what *deferments* means. Then, rewrite lines 44–46 in your own words.

_____

_____

_____

_____

Your TURN

BALANCING VIEWPOINTS

This article began with a typical textbook tone—objective and unbiased. However, in the section "The troops" (lines 39–59), the tone becomes more concerned and critical. Underline words and phrases that show this subjective tone.

from Declaration of Independence from the War in Vietnam

The war in Vietnam is connected to our war against poverty in America. The money and energy that used to be spent to help the poor is now going to the buildup in Vietnam. I see the war as an enemy of the poor, and I attack it as that enemy.

5 <u>The Vietnam War is doing more than destroying the hopes of the poor at home. It is also sending their sons, brothers, and husbands to fight and die.</u> Our society has crippled our young black men. Yet it sends them eight thousand miles away. They are fighting to free people in Southeast Asia, but they do not have

10 freedom here. Negro and white boys kill and die together, but, in this country, they cannot sit together in the same schools. I cannot be silent when I see how cruelly our poor people are being used.

I have taught angry young men that violence will not solve their problems. The best changes come about through nonviolent action.

15 But then they ask, What about Vietnam? They see that our own nation is using violence to solve its problems. Our nation is the greatest supplier of violence in the world today.

Somehow, this madness must stop. The poor of both Vietnam and America are suffering. I speak as a citizen of the world and for the

20 world which stands horrified at the path we have taken. I speak as an American to the leaders of our nation. We must take the first step to stop the war.

We must find new ways to speak for peace in Vietnam. This is the calling of the sons of God, and our brothers wait for our answer.

25 Now, let us dedicate ourselves to the struggle for a new world. Shall we say the odds are too great? Shall we tell them the struggle is too hard? Or will we be able to send a message of hope? Will we tell them that we share their goals, whatever the cost? The choice is ours, and though we might prefer not to make this choice, at this important

30 moment in human history, we *must* choose.

Balancing Viewpoints

Source Chart

When you begin to research a subject, it is helpful to keep track of the viewpoints you gather. One good way to do that is to keep a **Source Chart.** By recording information about your sources in the chart, you can make sure your research includes different viewpoints.

The two selections you just read are about the Vietnam War. However, they contain different viewpoints. Use the chart below to compare "The War Escalates" with the excerpt from "Declaration of Independence from the War in Vietnam." One column is already filled in for you.

	The War Escalates	Declaration of Independence from the War in Vietnam
1. Why does the author use **objective** information?	The author uses objective information to teach students about U.S. involvement in the Vietnam War.	
2. Why does the author use **subjective** information?	The author uses subjective information to criticize President Johnson's actions and U.S. draft policies.	
3. Does the writer have a **bias**? What is that **bias**?	Yes, the writer does have a bias against U.S. policy in Vietnam. The writer dislikes Congress giving the president war-making powers. The writer also dislikes the fact that minorities and poor people were more likely to be drafted and see combat than others.	

From The Tragedy of Julius Caesar, Act I, Scene 2

Literary Focus: Tragedy

Shakespeare tells us in the title of his play that *Julius Caesar* is a tragedy. A **tragedy** is a play, a novel, or other narrative that involves serious and important events and ends unhappily for the main character. Shakespeare's tragedies share these characteristics:

- The main character is often high ranking and dignified, not an ordinary man or woman.
- The main character has a **tragic flaw**—a defect in character or judgment—that directly causes the character's downfall.
- The play ends unhappily, with the death of the main character.

Reading Skill: Retelling

By **retelling** a story, or putting it in your own words, you can improve your understanding. When you say something in your own words, you have to think about the meaning. Some sections of this drama will be retold for you. You will be asked to retell other parts of the drama.

Into the Play

At the time this story takes place, Rome has been a republic, with elected leaders, for 450 years. However, Julius Caesar has been made dictator with supreme authority and command. Caesar, a successful general, is so popular that many Romans worry that the public will decide to crown him king. (Caesar himself was so swept up by his power that he erected a statue of himself. He named the statue "The Unconquerable God.") Some Romans don't want to have a king, so they decide to kill Caesar. History shows that their plan backfired. Rome was ruled for hundreds of years by kings who took the title *Caesar*. The word *Caesar* came to be a title of royalty, as in the Russian word *czar* and the German word *kaiser*.

The Tragedy of
JULIUS CAESAR

William Shakespeare

Act I, Scene 2

YOU NEED TO KNOW   The great general Julius Caesar has conquered many lands for the Roman Republic and has been made dictator. Some Romans fear Caesar's growing power and popularity with the people. In this scene, we learn that several Romans would like to get rid of Caesar.

Scene 2. *A public place.*

Enter CAESAR, ANTONY *(dressed for the race),* CALPHURNIA, PORTIA, DECIUS, CICERO, BRUTUS, CASSIUS, CASCA, *a* SOOTHSAYER;[1] *after them,* MARULLUS *and* FLAVIUS

Caesar.

1   Calphurnia!

Casca.   Peace, ho! Caesar speaks.

Caesar.   Calphurnia!

Calphurnia. Here, my lord.

Caesar.

Stand you directly in Antonius' way

When he doth run his course. Antonius!

5 **Antony.** Caesar, my lord?

Caesar.

Forget not in your speed, Antonius,

To touch Calphurnia; for our elders say

The barren, touchèd in this holy chase,

Shake off their sterile curse.

Antony.   I shall remember:

10   When Caesar says "Do this," it is performed.

Caesar.

Set on, and leave no ceremony out.

Soothsayer. Caesar!

Caesar. Ha! Who calls?

Casca.

Bid every noise be still; peace yet again!

---

1. **soothsayer:** a person who foretells the future.

Caesar.

15   Who is it in the press[2] that calls on me?

    I hear a tongue, shriller than all the music,

    Cry "Caesar." Speak; Caesar is turned to hear.

Soothsayer.

    Beware the ides of March.[3]

Caesar.   What man is that?

Brutus.

    A soothsayer bids you beware the ides of March.

IN OTHER WORDS   A crowd has gathered to watch a ceremonial race. A voice calls out to Caesar from the crowd. It is a fortuneteller telling Caesar to beware the ides of March.

Caesar.

20   Set him before me; let me see his face.

Cassius.

    Fellow, come from the throng; look upon Caesar.

Caesar.

    What say'st thou to me now? Speak once again.

Soothsayer.

    Beware the ides of March.

Caesar.

    He is a dreamer, let us leave him. Pass.

        [*Sennet.*[4] *Exeunt all except* BRUTUS *and* CASSIUS.]

Cassius.

25   Will you go see the order of the course?

Brutus. Not I.

Cassius. I pray you do.

Brutus.

    I am not gamesome: I do lack some part

    Of that quick spirit that is in Antony.

30   Let me not hinder, Cassius, your desires;

    I'll leave you.

---

2. **press:** crowd.
3. **ides** (ydz) **of March:** March 15.
4. **Sennet** (SEHN iht): flourish, or fanfare of trumpets announcing a ceremonial entrance or exit.

Here's HOW

RETELLING

In lines 15–19, the soothsayer calls out to Caesar and warns him of danger on a certain date—the ides of March. Caesar asks him to come forward, and the soothsayer repeats his warning to Caesar.

Your TURN

RETELLING

How does Caesar respond to the soothsayer in line 24?

_____

_____

_____

Your TURN

VOCABULARY

The word *pray* in line 27 can mean "to ask for" or "to speak to God." Which meaning do you think it has here?

_____

_____

_____

RETELLING

In lines 32–36, Cassius accuses Brutus of not treating him like a friend.

Your TURN

RETELLING

In lines 37–47, how does Brutus respond to Cassius?

_____

_____

_____

VOCABULARY

In line 37, Brutus says that he "veiled" his look. I know that a veil is a piece of fabric worn over the face. It hides the face. I don't think Brutus was really wearing a veil—I think that he is saying that his expression was like a veil that hid what was going on in his mind.

Cassius.

Brutus, I do observe you now of late;

I have not from your eyes that gentleness

And show of love as I was wont to have;

35   You bear too stubborn and too strange a hand[5]

Over your friend that loves you.

Brutus.   Cassius,

Be not deceived: if I have veiled my look,

I turn the trouble of my countenance

Merely[6] upon myself. Vexèd I am

40   Of late with passions of some difference,[7]

Conceptions only proper to myself,

Which give some soil,[8] perhaps, to my behaviors;

But let not therefore my good friends be grieved

(Among which number, Cassius, be you one)

45   Nor construe[9] any further my neglect

Than that poor Brutus, with himself at war,

Forgets the shows of love to other men.

IN OTHER WORDS   Caesar orders the fortuneteller to come forward and speak. However, Caesar does not take the warning seriously. The group heads off to the race, leaving Brutus and Cassius behind. Cassius says that Brutus, his friend, seems cold and unfriendly lately. Brutus explains that he simply has a lot on his mind.

Cassius.

Then, Brutus, I have much mistook your passion,[10]

By means whereof this breast of mine hath buried

50   Thoughts of great value, worthy cogitations.[11]

Tell me, good Brutus, can you see your face?

---

5. **You . . . hand:** Cassius is comparing Brutus's treatment of him to the way a trainer treats a horse.
6. **Merely:** wholly.
7. **passions of some difference:** conflicting feelings or emotions.
8. **give some soil:** stain or mar.
9. **construe** (KUHN stroo): to interpret.
10. **passion:** feeling.
11. **worthy cogitations** (KOJ uh TAY shuhnz): reflections of great value.

Brutus.

No, Cassius; for the eye sees not itself

But by reflection, by some other things.

Cassius.

'Tis just:[12]

55 And it is very much lamented, Brutus,

That you have no such mirrors as will turn

Your hidden worthiness into your eye,

That you might see your shadow.[13] I have heard

Where many of the best respect[14] in Rome

60 (Except immortal Caesar), speaking of Brutus,

And groaning underneath this age's yoke,

Have wished that noble Brutus had his eyes.

Brutus.

Into what dangers would you lead me, Cassius,

That you would have me seek into myself

65 For that which is not in me?

Cassius.

Therefore, good Brutus, be prepared to hear;

And since you know you cannot see yourself

So well as by reflection, I, your glass[15]

Will modestly discover to yourself

70 That of yourself which you yet know not of.

And be not jealous on[16] me, gentle Brutus:

Were I a common laughter,[17] or did use

To stale with ordinary oaths my love

To every new protester,[18] if you know

75 That I do fawn on men and hug them hard,

And after scandal them;[19] or if you know

That I profess myself in banqueting

To all the rout,[20] then hold me dangerous.

---

12. just: true.
13. shadow: reflection (of what others think of him).
14. respect: reputation.
15. glass: mirror.
16. jealous on: suspicious of.
17. common laughter: butt of a joke; object of mockery.
18. To stale . . . new protestor: In other words, if he swore to love everyone who came along.
19. scandal them: ruin them by gossip.
20. rout (rowt): common people, the mob.

RETELLING

In lines 48-53, Cassius asks Brutus if he can see himself. Brutus says that a person can only see a reflection of himself.

RETELLING

What is Cassius telling Brutus in lines 54–62?

_____

_____

_____

RETELLING

In lines 71-78, Cassius is saying that he is not the kind of person who flatters people to their faces and then tells stories about them behind their backs.

What does Brutus suspect the people are cheering about in lines 78–89? How does he feel about this?

_____

_____

_____

I looked up the word *aught* (line 85) in a dictionary and found out that it means "anything." When I substitute "anything" for "aught," that speech keeps the same meaning.

You can see from the footnote that the word *favor* in line 91 is used with *outward* to mean "appearance." What other meaning of *favor* do you know?

_____

_____

_____

IN OTHER WORDS   Cassius begins to flatter Brutus, suggesting that many in Rome consider him Caesar's equal. He says he wishes that Brutus could see himself as others see him. Brutus asks why Cassius is urging such dangerous ideas. Cassius tries to persuade Brutus to trust him.

[*Flourish*[21] *and shout.*]

Brutus.

What means this shouting? I do fear the people

Choose Caesar for their king.

80　**Cassius.**　　　　　　　　　　Ay, do you fear it?

Then must I think you would not have it so.

Brutus.

I would not, Cassius, yet I love him well.

But wherefore do you hold me here so long?

What is it that you would impart to me?

85　If it be aught toward the general good,

Set honor in one eye and death i' th' other,

And I will look on both indifferently;[22]

For let the gods so speed me, as I love

The name of honor more than I fear death.

Cassius.

90　I know that virtue to be in you, Brutus,

As well as I do know your outward favor.[23]

Well, honor is the subject of my story.

I cannot tell what you and other men

Think of this life, but for my single self,

95　I had as lief[24] not be, as live to be

In awe of such a thing as I myself.

I was born free as Caesar; so were you:

We both have fed as well, and we can both

Endure the winter's cold as well as he:

---

21. **Flourish** (FLUR ihsh): brief, elaborate music of trumpets.
22. **indifferently:** impartially; fairly.
23. **outward favor:** appearance.
24. **as lief** (leef): just as soon.

100 For once, upon a raw and gusty day,

The troubled Tiber chafing with²⁵ her shores,

Caesar said to me "Dar'st thou, Cassius, now

Leap in with me into this angry flood,

And swim to yonder point?" Upon the word,

105 Accout'red as I was, I plungèd in

And bade him follow: so indeed he did.

The torrent roared, and we did buffet it

With lusty sinews, throwing it aside

And stemming it with hearts of controversy.²⁶

IN OTHER WORDS   Offstage, there is the sound of trumpets and shouting. Brutus fears that the noise means the people are making Julius Caesar king. (Rome is a republic and has no king.) Brutus says that he is loyal to Caesar, but would not want him to be king. He asks Cassius what he wants. Cassius replies that in Rome all free men are equal citizens, Caesar included.

110 But ere we could arrive the point proposed,

Caesar cried "Help me, Cassius, or I sink!"

I, as Aeneas,²⁷ our great ancestor,

Did from the flames of Troy upon his shoulder

The old Anchises bear, so from the waves of Tiber

115 Did I the tired Caesar. And this man

Is now become a god, and Cassius is

A wretched creature, and must bend his body

If Caesar carelessly but nod on him.

He had a fever when he was in Spain,

120 And when the fit was on him, I did mark

How he did shake; 'tis true, this god did shake.

His coward lips did from their color fly,

---

25. **chafing** (CHAYF ihng) **with:** raging against (the river was rough with waves and currents).
26. **hearts of controversy** (KON truh vur see): hearts full of aggressive feelings, or fighting spirit.
27. **Aeneas** (ih NEE uhs): legendary forefather of the Roman people who, in Virgil's *Aeneid*, fled from the burning city of Troy carrying his old father on his back. (In many accounts of the legend, Romulus and Remus were descendants of Aeneas.)

Your TURN

VOCABULARY

In lines 100–109, Cassius tells how he rescued Caesar from the river. Cassius describes the river, using words that make the river sound like an animal or a person. For example, in line 107, Cassius says that the "torrent roared." Circle at least two other words that describe the river as a person or animal.

Your TURN

VOCABULARY

The word *bear* can mean "a big, shaggy animal," "to carry," or "move to the side." Which meaning do you think *bear* has in line 114? Explain your answer.

_____

_____

_____

_____

Here's HOW

RETELLING

In lines 110–118, Cassius says that he rescued Caesar from drowning in the river Tiber. But now Caesar is powerful, like a god, and Cassius must bow down before him—even at the nod of Caesar's head.

RETELLING

What story does Cassius tell about Caesar in lines 119–124?

_____

_____

_____

RETELLING

In lines 135–138, Cassius says that Caesar has become as powerful as a giant. Men like Cassius are small in comparison.

RETELLING

In lines 139–141, whom does Cassius blame for his and Brutus's troubles?

_____

_____

_____

And that same eye whose bend doth awe the world

Did lose his luster; I did hear him groan;

125   Ay, and that tongue of his, that bade the Romans

Mark him and write his speeches in their books,

Alas, it cried, "Give me some drink, Titinius,"

As a sick girl. Ye gods! It doth amaze me,

A man of such a feeble temper should

130   So get the start of the majestic world,

And bear the palm[28] alone.

[*Shout. Flourish.*]

Brutus. Another general shout?

I do believe that these applauses are

For some new honors that are heaped on Caesar.

Cassius.

135   Why, man, he doth bestride the narrow world

Like a Colossus,[29] and we petty men

Walk under his huge legs and peep about

To find ourselves dishonorable graves.

Men at some time are masters of their fates:

140   The fault, dear Brutus, is not in our stars,[30]

But in ourselves, that we are underlings.

IN OTHER WORDS   Cassius tells two stories about his days in the army under Caesar. Both stories show Caesar as weak. Caesar, he says, is no better a man than he is; in fact, he is less of one. Why should Caesar be like a god, while he and Brutus seem small and unimportant? Why should they allow Caesar to have power over them?

---

28. **bear the palm:** hold the palm branch, an award given to a victorious general.
29. **Colossus** (kuh LOS uhs): huge statue of Helios that was said to straddle the entrance to the harbor at Rhodes, an island in the Aegean Sea. The statue, so huge that ships passed under its legs, was one of the Seven Wonders of the Ancient World. It was destroyed by an earthquake in 224 B.C.
30. **stars:** Elizabethans believed that one's life was governed by the stars or constellation one was born under.

Brutus and Caesar: what should be in that "Caesar"?

Why should that name be sounded more than yours?

Write them together, yours is as fair a name;

145 Sound them, it doth become the mouth as well;

Weigh them, it is as heavy; conjure with 'em,

"Brutus" will start a spirit as soon as "Caesar."

Now, in the names of all the gods at once,

Upon what meat doth this our Caesar feed,

150 That he is grown so great? Age, thou art shamed!

Rome, thou hast lost the breed of noble bloods!

When went there by an age, since the great flood,³¹

But it was famed with more than with one man?

When could they say (till now) that talked of Rome,

155 That her wide walks encompassed but one man?

Now is it Rome indeed, and room³² enough,

When there is in it but one only man.

O, you and I have heard our fathers say,

There was a Brutus once that would have brooked³³

160 Th' eternal devil to keep his state in Rome

As easily as a king.³⁴

Brutus.

That you do love me, I am nothing jealous;

What you would work me to, I have some aim;³⁵

How I have thought of this, and of these times,

165 I shall recount hereafter. For this present,

I would not so (with love I might entreat you)

Be any further moved. What you have said

I will consider; what you have to say

I will with patience hear, and find a time

170 Both meet³⁶ to hear and answer such high things.

Till then, my noble friend, chew upon this:

RETELLING

In lines 148-157, Cassius is complaining that Romans should be ashamed of letting one man become so powerful that he is more important than Rome itself.

TRAGEDY

In lines 162-170, Brutus tells Cassius that he knows Cassius wants to get rid of Caesar. Brutus says he is willing to listen to Cassius and will think about what Cassius has said.

VOCABULARY

Look in the footnote for one meaning of the word *meet* (line 170). What other meaning of *meet* do you know?

_____

_____

---

31. the great flood: flood sent by Zeus to drown all the wicked people on Earth. Only the faithful couple Deucalion and Pyrrha were saved.

32. Rome . . . room: a pun; both words were pronounced room in Shakespeare's day.

33. brooked: put up with.

34. Th' eternal . . . king: This refers to the ancestor of Brutus who, in the sixth century B.C., helped to expel the last king from Rome and set up the Republic.

35. aim: idea.

36. meet: appropriate.

TRAGEDY

Often, the first act of a tragedy introduces the characters and their conflicts. What conflict has developed in this scene?

_____

_____

_____

VOCABULARY

In line 184, Brutus uses the word *train*. What meaning does *train* have in that line? Explain your answer.

_____

_____

_____

Brutus had rather be a villager

Than to repute himself a son of Rome

Under these hard conditions as this time

Is like to lay upon us.

175 **Cassius.**   I am glad

That my weak words have struck but thus much show

Of fire from Brutus.

IN OTHER WORDS   Cassius says there is no reason that Brutus should not be as great as Caesar. He reminds Brutus of his ancestor, who helped get rid of the last king of Rome and make their nation a republic. Brutus replies that he trusts Cassius's friendship. He has some idea of what Cassius wants him to do, but he is not ready to give an answer. He will think about what Cassius has said.

[*Enter* CAESAR *and his* TRAIN.]

Brutus.

The games are done, and Caesar is returning.

Cassius.

As they pass by, pluck Casca by the sleeve,

180   And he will (after his sour fashion) tell you

What hath proceeded worthy note today.

Brutus.

I will do so. But look you, Cassius,

The angry spot doth glow on Caesar's brow,

And all the rest look like a chidden[37] train:

185   Calphurnia's cheek is pale, and Cicero

Looks with such ferret[38] and such fiery eyes

As we have seen him in the Capitol,

Being crossed in conference by some senators.

Cassius.

Casca will tell us what the matter is.

---

37. **chidden** (CHIHD uhn): rebuked; corrected.
38. **ferret:** weasel-like animal, usually considered crafty.

190   **Caesar.** Antonius.

Antony. Caesar?

Caesar.

Let me have men about me that are fat,

Sleek-headed men, and such as sleep a-nights.

Yond Cassius has a lean and hungry look;

195   He thinks too much: such men are dangerous.

Antony.

Fear him not, Caesar, he's not dangerous;

He is a noble Roman, and well given.[39]

Caesar.

Would he were fatter! But I fear him not.

Yet if my name were liable to fear,

200   I do not know the man I should avoid

So soon as that spare Cassius. He reads much,

He is a great observer, and he looks

Quite through the deeds of men.[40] He loves no plays,

As thou dost, Antony; he hears no music;

205   Seldom he smiles, and smiles in such a sort[41]

As if he mocked himself, and scorned his spirit

That could be moved to smile at anything.

Such men as he be never at heart's ease

Whiles they behold a greater than themselves,

210   And therefore are they very dangerous.

I rather tell thee what is to be feared

Than what I fear; for always I am Caesar.

Come on my right hand, for this ear is deaf,

And tell me truly what thou think'st of him.

[*Sennet. Exeunt* CAESAR *and his* TRAIN.]

Here's HOW

RETELLING

In lines 192–195, Caesar says he doesn't trust men such as Cassius who are ambitious and dissatisfied. He would rather be surrounded by men who are content with what they have.

Your TURN

RETELLING

What does Caesar say about fear in lines 198–201?

_____

_____

_____

Your TURN

TRAGEDY

In lines 208–214, Caesar tells what he thinks of Cassius. What do his words tell us about Caesar's character?

_____

_____

_____

---

39. well given: well disposed to support Caesar.

40. he looks . . . of men: In other words, he looks through what men do to search out their feelings and motives.

41. sort: manner.

IN OTHER WORDS Caesar and the others return. Cassius suggests that Brutus take Casca aside and find out what's been happening. Brutus notices that neither Caesar nor his followers look happy.

Caesar sees the two men, and tells Antony that Cassius is ambitious and dissatisfied, and therefore dangerous. Antony tells him not to be afraid—Cassius is a loyal supporter. Caesar says that he is not afraid of anyone, but if he were to be afraid, he would fear Cassius.

Casca.

215 You pulled me by the cloak; would you speak with me?

Brutus.

Ay, Casca; tell us what hath chanced today,

That Caesar looks so sad.[42]

Casca.

Why, you were with him, were you not?

Brutus.

I should not then ask Casca what had chanced.

220 **Casca.** Why, there was a crown offered him; and being

offered him, he put it by[43] with the back of his hand,

thus; and then the people fell a-shouting.

Brutus. What was the second noise for?

Casca. Why, for that too.

Cassius.

225 They shouted thrice; what was the last cry for?

Casca. Why, for that too.

Brutus. Was the crown offered him thrice?

Casca. Ay, marry,[44] was't, and he put it by thrice, every

time gentler than other; and at every putting-by mine

230 honest neighbors shouted.

Cassius.

Who offered him the crown?

---

42. **sad:** serious.
43. **put it by:** pushed it aside.
44. **marry:** a mild oath meaning "by the Virgin Mary."

Casca. Why, Antony.

Brutus.

Tell us the manner of it, gentle Casca.

IN OTHER WORDS Brutus stops Casca and asks what made Caesar look so unhappy. Casca explains that Antony offered Caesar a crown in front of the crowd three times, and Caesar refused it three times. The shouts they heard were the crowd cheering Caesar's refusal to be king.

Casca. I can as well be hanged as tell the manner of it:
235   it was mere foolery; I did not mark it. I saw Mark
     Antony offer him a crown—yet 'twas not a crown
     neither, 'twas one of these coronets[45]—and, as I told
     you, he put it by once; but for all that, to my thinking,
     he would fain[46] have had it. Then he offered it to him
240   again; then he put it by again; but to my thinking, he
     was very loath to lay his fingers off it. And then he
     offered it the third time. He put it the third time by;
     and still as he refused it, the rabblement hooted, and
     clapped their chopt[47] hands, and threw up their
245   sweaty nightcaps,[48] and uttered such a deal of
     stinking breath because Caesar refused the crown,
     that it had, almost, choked Caesar; for he swounded[49]
     and fell down at it. And for mine own part, I durst not
     laugh, for fear of opening my lips and receiving the
250   bad air.

RETELLING

In lines 234–248, Casca says that offering the crown to Caesar was putting on a show, and Caesar had to go along with it and reject the crown. However, Casca believes that Caesar really wanted to accept the crown—he wanted to be king.

TRAGEDY

What do we learn about Casca in lines 241–250?

_____

_____

_____

_____

---

45. coronets (KAWR uh NEHTZ): small crowns.
46. fain (fayn): happily.
47. chopt: chapped (raw and rough from hard work and the weather).
48. nightcaps: Casca is mockingly referring to the hats of the workingmen.
49. swounded (SWOON dihd): swooned or fainted.

Here's HOW

RETELLING

In lines 257–261, Casca says that Caesar is nothing more than an actor, doing whatever makes the crowd happy.

Your TURN

RETELLING

What does Casca say about Caesar in lines 269–275?

_____

_____

_____

Cassius.

But, soft,[50] I pray you; what, did Caesar swound?

Casca. He fell down in the market place, and foamed at mouth, and was speechless.

Brutus.

'Tis very like he hath the falling-sickness.[51]

Cassius.

255   No, Caesar hath it not; but you, and I,

And honest Casca, we have the falling-sickness.

Casca. I know not what you mean by that, but I am sure Caesar fell down. If the tag-rag people[52] did not clap him and hiss him, according as he pleased and

260   displeased them, as they use to do the players in the theater, I am no true man.

Brutus.

What said he when he came unto himself?

Casca. Marry, before he fell down, when he perceived the common herd was glad he refused the crown, he

265   plucked me ope[53] his doublet[54] and offered them his throat to cut. An[55] I had been a man of any occupation,[56] if I would not have taken him at a word, I would I might go to hell among the rogues. And so he fell. When he came to himself again, he

270   said, if he had done or said anything amiss, he desired their worships to think it was his infirmity. Three or four wenches,[57] where I stood, cried "Alas, good soul!" and forgave him with all their hearts; but there's no heed to be taken of them; if Caesar had

275   stabbed their mothers, they would have done no less.

Brutus.

And after that, he came thus sad away?

---

50. **soft:** wait a minute.
51. **falling-sickness:** old term for the disease we now call epilepsy, which is marked by seizures and momentary loss of consciousness.
52. **tag-rag people:** contemptuous reference to the commoners in the crowd.
53. **plucked me ope:** plucked open.
54. **doublet:** close-fitting jacket.
55. **An:** if.
56. **man of any occupation:** working man.
57. **wenches:** girls or young women.

124   HOLT ADAPTED READER

Casca. Ay.

Cassius.

Did Cicero say anything?

Casca. Ay, he spoke Greek.

280 **Cassius.** To what effect?

Casca. Nay, an I tell you that, I'll ne'er look you i' th'
face again. But those that understood him smiled at
one another and shook their heads; but for mine own
part, it was Greek to me. I could tell you more news
285 too: Marullus and Flavius, for pulling scarfs off
Caesar's images, are put to silence.[58] Fare you well.
There was more foolery yet, if I could remember it.

Cassius. Will you sup with me tonight, Casca?

Casca. No, I am promised forth.[59]

290 **Cassius.** Will you dine with me tomorrow?

Casca. Ay, if I be alive, and your mind hold, and your
dinner worth the eating.

Cassius. Good; I will expect you.

Casca. Do so. Farewell, both. [*Exit.*]

Brutus.

295 What a blunt fellow is this grown to be!
He was quick mettle[60] when he went to school.

Cassius.

So is he now in execution
Of any bold or noble enterprise,
However he puts on this tardy form.[61]

---

58. **put to silence:** silenced, perhaps being dismissed from their positions as tribunes or by being exiled.
59. **forth:** previously (he has other plans).
60. **quick mettle:** lively of disposition.
61. **tardy form:** sluggish appearance.

Here's HOW

RETELLING

In lines 278–284, Cassius asks how Cicero, Caesar's rival, reacted to what happened. Casca says he doesn't know because Cicero spoke in Greek, which Casca doesn't understand. Casca says that those who did understand Greek smiled at one another and shook their heads.

Your TURN

RETELLING

What do Brutus and Cassius say about Casca in lines 295–299?

_____

_____

RETELLING

In lines 300-302, Cassius says Casca covers up his intelligence with a rough manner, pretending to be ordinary. Because of this, people listen to him and accept what he says.

RETELLING

In lines 308–312, what does Cassius say about Brutus?

_____

_____

_____

300 This rudeness[62] is a sauce to his good wit,[63]

Which gives men stomach to disgest[64] his words

With better appetite.

IN OTHER WORDS Cassius asks how Cicero reacted to all this. Casca says Cicero made a comment in Greek, so he didn't understand it. He also says that two opponents of Caesar have been silenced. Cassius invites Casca to dinner, and Casca agrees to come the next day. Then Casca leaves, and Cassius tells Brutus that Casca acts so rude to disguise his sharp intelligence.

Brutus.

And so it is. For this time I will leave you.

Tomorrow, if you please to speak with me,

305 I will come home to you; or if you will,

Come home to me, and I will wait for you.

Cassius.

I will do so. Till then, think of the world.[65]

[*Exit* BRUTUS.]

Well, Brutus, thou art noble; yet I see

Thy honorable mettle may be wrought

310 From that it is disposed;[66] therefore it is meet

That noble minds keep ever with their likes;

For who so firm that cannot be seduced?

Caesar doth bear me hard,[67] but he loves Brutus.

If I were Brutus now and he were Cassius,

315 He should not humor[68] me. I will this night,

In several hands,[69] in at his windows throw,

---

62. **rudeness:** rough manner.
63. **wit:** intelligence.
64. **disgest:** to digest.
65. **the world:** the state of affairs in Rome.
66. **Thy honorable . . . disposed:** In other words, he may be persuaded against his better nature to join the conspirators.
67. **bear me hard:** has a grudge (hard feelings) against me.
68. **humor:** to influence by flattery.
69. **hands:** varieties of handwriting.

As if they came from several citizens,

Writings, all tending to the great opinion

That Rome holds of his name; wherein obscurely

320 Caesar's ambition shall be glancèd at.[70]

And after this, let Caesar seat him sure;[71]

For we will shake him, or worse days endure. [*Exit.*]

RETELLING

In lines 315–320, Cassius says that he's going to write fake letters to Brutus to convince him that the people want him to be in power instead of Caesar.

IN OTHER WORDS   Brutus says he and Cassius will continue their talk the next day. He leaves. Cassius, alone, says he will send Brutus anonymous notes in several different handwritings, flattering Brutus further, and hinting that other Romans see Caesar as too ambitious.

---

70. **glancèd at:** touched on.
71. **seat him sure:** make his position secure.

Tragedy

A **tragedy** is a play, a novel, or other narrative that involves serious and important events and ends unhappily for the main character. In Act I, the main characters and their conflicts are introduced. Act I also establishes the setting and provides background information.

Fill in the categories in the graphic organizer below with the information you have learned in Act I.

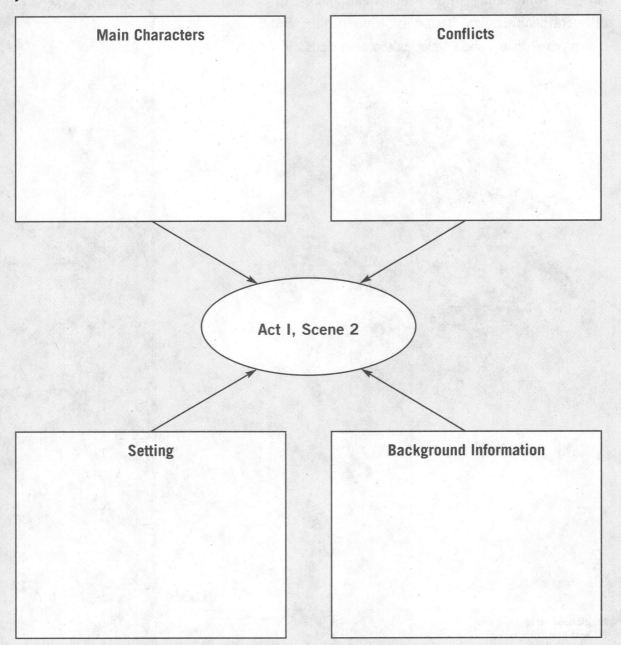

Main Characters

Conflicts

Act I, Scene 2

Setting

Background Information

Vocabulary Development

How to Own a Word

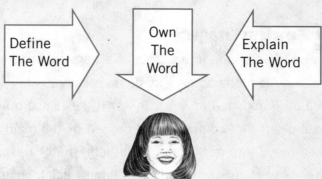

Carefully read each word's definition, explanation, and sample sentence. Then, write a sentence of your own using that word.

1. veiled (vayld): **Definition:** hid from sight **Explanation:** A veil is a piece of thin fabric worn over the face, hiding it. **Sample Sentence:** The huge brim of the woman's hat *veiled* her eyes.	**My Sentence:**
2. bear: **Definition:** to carry **Explanation:** Bear can also mean to move to one side, like "bear right here," or it can mean an animal. **Sample Sentence:** The new bridge will have to *bear* the load of hundreds of cars.	**My Sentence:**
3. sad: **Definition:** serious **Explanation:** Sad can mean "not happy" or "full of sorrow." But another meaning is "extremely bad" or "serious." **Sample Sentence:** The young man looked at the flat tire on his car and said, "This is a *sad* situation."	**My Sentence:**

From The Tragedy of Julius Caesar, Act III, Scene 2

Literary Focus: Tragedy

Certain events usually happen in each act of a tragedy. As you
learned earlier, the main characters, conflicts, setting, and
background are all introduced in Act I. In Act II, suspense builds
as events create a series of complications caused by the main
characters when they try to resolve their conflicts. In Act III (part
of which you're about to read), the **crisis,** or **turning point,** occurs.
This is the dramatic and tense moment when the main character
makes the choice that determines the rest of the play's action.

Reading Skill: Understanding Persuasion

Persuasive speakers want to change the way their listeners think or to
get their listeners to carry out an action. The persuasive techniques
these people use are emotional appeals, powerful words, repetition,
and props. Props are movable objects such as a flag or a poster.

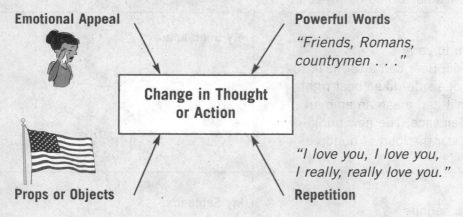

Emotional Appeal

Powerful Words

"Friends, Romans, countrymen . . ."

Change in Thought or Action

"I love you, I love you, I really, really love you."

Props or Objects

Repetition

Into the Play

This scene from *The Tragedy of Julius Caesar* is one of the great
examples of a persuasive speech. Antony, standing over Caesar's
bloody corpse, completely changes the mood of the mob.

FROM

The Tragedy of
JULIUS CAESAR

Act III, Scene 2

YOU NEED TO KNOW   Cassius succeeds in persuading Brutus to join a plan to kill Caesar. Brutus carries out the assassination of Caesar on the ides of March,[1] just as the soothsayer[2] foretold. Over Cassius's objections, Brutus gives Antony permission to speak to the crowd at Caesar's funeral. However, Cassius makes Antony promise to say nothing negative about the conspirators—the men who planned the assassination.

A crowd of common people fill the forum (marketplace) demanding to know why their hero Caesar has been killed. Half the crowd goes off with Cassius to hear his explanation; Brutus stays to speak to the rest.

Scene 2. *The Forum.*

Enter BRUTUS *and goes into the pulpit, and* CASSIUS, *with the* PLEBEIANS.[3]

Plebeians.

1   We will be satisfied! Let us be satisfied!

Brutus.

Then follow me, and give me audience, friends.

Cassius, go you into the other street

And part the numbers.

5   Those that will hear me speak, let 'em stay here;

Those that will follow Cassius, go with him;

And public reasons shall be renderèd

Of Caesar's death.

First Plebeian.   I will hear Brutus speak.

Second Plebeian.

I will hear Cassius, and compare their reasons,

10   When severally we hear them renderèd.

[*Exit* CASSIUS, *with some of the* PLEBEIANS.]

Third Plebeian.

The noble Brutus is ascended. Silence!

---

1. **ides** (ydz) **of March:** March 15.
2. **soothsayer:** a person who foretells the future.
3. **Plebeians** (plih BEE uhnz): the common people.

Brutus. Be patient till the last.

Romans, countrymen, and lovers, hear me for my cause, and be silent, that you may hear. Believe me

15 for mine honor, and have respect to mine honor, that you may believe. Censure[4] me in your wisdom, and awake your senses,[5] that you may the better judge. If there be any in this assembly, any dear friend of Caesar's, to him I say that Brutus' love to Caesar

20 was no less than his. If then that friend demand why Brutus rose against Caesar, this is my answer: Not that I loved Caesar less, but that I loved Rome more. Had you rather Caesar were living, and die all slaves, than that Caesar were dead, to live all free men? As

25 Caesar loved me, I weep for him; as he was fortunate, I rejoice at it; as he was valiant, I honor him; but, as he was ambitious, I slew him. There is tears, for his love; joy, for his fortune; honor, for his valor; and death, for his ambition. Who is here so base, that

30 would be a bondman?[6] If any, speak; for him have I offended. Who is here so rude,[7] that would not be a Roman? If any, speak; for him have I offended. Who is here so vile, that will not love his country? If any, speak; for him have I offended. I pause for a

35 reply.

All. None, Brutus, none!

Brutus.

Then none have I offended. I have done no more to Caesar than you shall do to Brutus. The question of his death is enrolled[8] in the Capitol; his glory not

40 extenuated,[9] wherein he was worthy, nor his offenses enforced,[10] for which he suffered death.

---

4. **censure** (SEHN shuhr): judge.
5. **senses:** reasoning powers.
6. **bondman:** slave.
7. **rude:** rough and uncivilized.
8. In other words, there is a record of the reasons he was killed.
9. **extenuated** (ehk STEHN yu ay tehd): lessened.
10. **enforced** (ehn FOHRST): exaggerated.

Here's HOW

UNDERSTANDING PERSUASION

Brutus uses powerful words and repeats them over and over to persuade the plebeians that it was all right to kill Caesar. For example, in line 15, he repeats the words *mine honor* twice. He repeats the word *friend* several times as well.

Your TURN

UNDERSTANDING PERSUASION

One way to change the way people think or act is to use powerful words. Re-read Brutus's speech (lines 13–35), and draw a circle around at least five powerful words that Brutus has repeated several times. An example would be the word *loved,* which Brutus uses four times in his speech.

Your TURN

TRAGEDY

Review the characteristics of a tragic hero on page 110. In what ways does Brutus fit the role of a tragic hero?

_____

_____

_____

[*Enter* MARK ANTONY, *with Caesar's body.*]

Here comes his body, mourned by Mark Antony, who, though he had no hand in his death, shall receive the benefit of his dying, a place in the commonwealth, as
45 which of you shall not? With this I depart, that, as I slew my best lover for the good of Rome, I have the same dagger for myself, when it shall please my country to need my death.

All. Live, Brutus! Live, live!

First Plebeian.
50 Bring him with triumph home unto his house.

Second Plebeian.
Give him a statue with his ancestors.

Third Plebeian.
Let him be Caesar.

Fourth Plebeian. Caesar's better parts[11]
Shall be crowned in Brutus.

First Plebeian.
55 We'll bring him to his house with shouts and clamors.

Brutus. My countrymen—

Second Plebeian.   Peace! Silence! Brutus speaks.

First Plebeian. Peace, ho!

Brutus.
Good countrymen, let me depart alone,
And, for my sake, stay here with Antony.
60 Do grace to Caesar's corpse, and grace his speech[12]
Tending to Caesar's glories, which Mark Antony
By our permission, is allowed to make.
I do entreat you, not a man depart,
Save I alone, till Antony have spoke. [*Exit.*]

First Plebeian.
65 Stay, ho! And let us hear Mark Antony.

---

11. **better parts:** better qualities.
12. **grace his speech:** listen respectfully to Antony's funeral oration.

Third Plebeian.

Let him go up into the public chair;[13]

We'll hear him. Noble Antony, go up.

Antony.

For Brutus' sake, I am beholding to you.

Fourth Plebeian.

What does he say of Brutus?

Third Plebeian.   He says, for Brutus' sake,

70   He finds himself beholding to us all.

Fourth Plebeian.

'Twere best he speak no harm of Brutus here!

First Plebeian.

This Caesar was a tyrant.

Third Plebeian.   Nay, that's certain.

We are blest that Rome is rid of him.

Second Plebeian.

Peace! Let us hear what Antony can say.

Antony.

75   You gentle Romans—

All.   Peace, ho! Let us hear him.

Antony.

Friends, Romans, countrymen, lend me your ears;

I come to bury Caesar, not to praise him.

IN OTHER WORDS   Brutus leaves, and Antony is
ready to speak. The crowd has turned entirely against Caesar
and in favor of Brutus. Antony faces a hostile crowd. He has
promised Brutus to say nothing against Caesar's killers. He
promises the crowd that he does not intend to praise Caesar.

The evil that men do lives after them,

The good is oft interrèd with their bones;

80   So let it be with Caesar. The noble Brutus

Hath told you Caesar was ambitious.

---

13. **public chair:** pulpit or rostrum.

UNDERSTANDING PERSUASION

One of the ways to persuade people to do as you want is to use powerful words that bring up strong emotions. In line 76, Antony begins his speech with the words, "Friends, . . . " Circle the three powerful words in line 76 that help break down the crowd's hostility.

VOCABULARY

In line 76, the phrase "lend me your ears" is an example of idiomatic, or not literally true, language. Antony cannot possibly be asking his audience to take off their ears and loan them to him. What does Antony really want when he asks the plebeians to "lend me your ears"?

_____

_____

_____

_____

UNDERSTANDING PERSUASION

Why do you think Antony repeats the phrase "Brutus is an honorable man" so many times? What does he really want the crowd to believe about Brutus?

_____

_____

_____

UNDERSTANDING PERSUASION

In lines 111–113, draw a line under the words that show that the plebeians are changing how they think about Brutus.

If it were so, it was a grievous fault,

And grievously hath Caesar answered[14] it.

Here, under leave of Brutus and the rest

85   (For Brutus is an honorable man,

So are they all, all honorable men),

Come I to speak in Caesar's funeral.

He was my friend, faithful and just to me;

But Brutus says he was ambitious,

90   And Brutus is an honorable man.

He hath brought many captives home to Rome,

Whose ransoms did the general coffers[15] fill;

Did this in Caesar seem ambitious?

When that the poor have cried, Caesar hath wept;

95   Ambition should be made of sterner stuff.

Yet Brutus says he was ambitious;

And Brutus is an honorable man.

You all did see that on the Lupercal

I thrice presented him a kingly crown,

100   Which he did thrice refuse. Was this ambition?

Yet Brutus says he was ambitious;

And sure he is an honorable man.

I speak not to disprove what Brutus spoke,

But here I am to speak what I do know.

105   You all did love him once, not without cause;

What cause withholds you then to mourn for him?

O judgment, thou art fled to brutish beasts,

And men have lost their reason! Bear with me;

My heart is in the coffin there with Caesar,

110   And I must pause till it come back to me.

First Plebeian.

Methinks there is much reason in his sayings.

Second Plebeian.

If thou consider rightly of the matter,

Caesar has had great wrong.

---

14. **answered:** paid the penalty for.
15. **general coffers** (KAWF uhrz): public funds.

Third Plebeian. Has he, masters?

> I fear there will a worse come in his place.

Fourth Plebeian.

115 > Marked ye his words? He would not take the crown,
> Therefore 'tis certain he was not ambitious.

First Plebeian.

> If it be found so, some will dear abide it.[16]

Second Plebeian.

> Poor soul, his eyes are red as fire with weeping.

Third Plebeian.

> There's not a nobler man in Rome than Antony.

Fourth Plebeian.

120 > Now mark him, he begins again to speak.

Antony's speech is filled with irony—saying one thing but meaning the opposite. For example, he says that Brutus and the other assassins are honorable men, though he certainly believes the opposite. While pretending to agree with Brutus, Antony questions whether Caesar's actions were really overly ambitious. Antony reminds the crowd of all the good Caesar did for Rome. He scolds the people for forgetting their love for Caesar so quickly. The crowd, easily persuaded, turns again in favor of Caesar and Antony.

Antony.

> But yesterday the word of Caesar might
> Have stood against the world; now lies he there,
> And none so poor to[17] do him reverence.
> O masters! If I were disposed to stir

125 > Your hearts and minds to mutiny and rage,
> I should do Brutus wrong and Cassius wrong,
> Who, you all know, are honorable men.
> I will not do them wrong; I rather choose

---

16. **dear abide it:** pay dearly for it.
17. **so poor to:** so low in rank as to.

Your
TURN

UNDERSTANDING PERSUASION

What persuasive technique is Antony using when he holds up Caesar's will and shows it to the plebeians?

_____

_____

_____

Your
TURN

VOCABULARY

The word *meet* in line 144 can mean "to come together," "fitting and proper," or "a gathering." Underline the meaning it has here. Then, on the lines below, write a sentence using *meet* with one of its other meanings.

_____

_____

_____

_____

_____

To wrong the dead, to wrong myself and you,

130 Than I will wrong such honorable men.

But here's a parchment with the seal of Caesar;

I found it in his closet; 'tis his will.

Let but the commons hear this testament,

Which, pardon me, I do not mean to read,

135 And they would go and kiss dead Caesar's wounds,

And dip their napkins[18] in his sacred blood;

Yea, beg a hair of him for memory,

And dying, mention it within their wills,

Bequeathing it as a rich legacy

140 Unto their issue.[19]

Fourth Plebeian.

We'll hear the will; read it, Mark Antony.

All. The will, the will! We will hear Caesar's will!

IN OTHER WORDS   Antony says he would never want to stir up the crowd against the "honorable" Cassius and Brutus. He brings out Caesar's will. However, he says that he won't read it, because it would make their grief over Caesar's death even more unbearable. Antony tells the crowd they are Caesar's heirs. Naturally, the crowd insists on hearing what is in Caesar's will.

Antony.

Have patience, gentle friends, I must not read it.

It is not meet you know how Caesar loved you.

145 You are not wood, you are not stones, but men;

And being men, hearing the will of Caesar,

It will inflame you, it will make you mad.

'Tis good you know not that you are his heirs;

For if you should, O, what would come of it?

---

18. **napkins:** handkerchiefs.
19. **issue:** children; heirs.

Fourth Plebeian.

150   Read the will! We'll hear it, Antony!

    You shall read us the will, Caesar's will!

Antony.

    Will you be patient? Will you stay awhile?

    I have o'ershot myself[20] to tell you of it.

    I fear I wrong the honorable men

155   Whose daggers have stabbed Caesar; I do fear it.

Fourth Plebeian.

    They were traitors. Honorable men!

All. The will! The testament!

Second Plebeian. They were villains, murderers! The

    will! Read the will!

Antony.

160   You will compel me then to read the will?

    Then make a ring about the corpse of Caesar,

    And let me show you him that made the will.

    Shall I descend? And will you give me leave?

All. Come down.

Second Plebeian. Descend.

    [ANTONY *comes down.*]

165 **Third Plebeian.** You shall have leave.

Fourth Plebeian. A ring! Stand round.

First Plebeian.

    Stand from the hearse, stand from the body!

Second Plebeian.

    Room for Antony, most noble Antony!

Antony.

    Nay, press not so upon me; stand far off.

170 **All.** Stand back! Room! Bear back.

Antony.

    If you have tears, prepare to shed them now.

    You all do know this mantle; I remember

    The first time ever Caesar put it on:

---

20. o'ershot myself: gone farther than I intended.

Your TURN

UNDERSTANDING PERSUASION

In lines 153–155, underline what Antony says when he really means, "I hate and am not afraid of the dishonorable assassins and traitors who killed Caesar."

Your TURN

UNDERSTANDING PERSUASION

Now, draw a circle around the words that the plebeians shout that show that Antony's persuasive techniques are successful.

Here's HOW

UNDERSTANDING PERSUASION

In lines 171–180, Antony uses another prop to stir up the emotions of the crowd—poor Caesar's bloody mantle, or cloak.

Your TURN

VOCABULARY

What do you think the word *rent* in line 177 means? Explain your answer.

_____

_____

_____

'Twas on a summer's evening, in his tent,

175   That day he overcame the Nervii.[21]

Look, in this place ran Cassius' dagger through;

See what a rent the envious[22] Casca made;

Through this the well-belovèd Brutus stabbed,

And as he plucked his cursèd steel away,

180 Mark how the blood of Caesar followed it,

As rushing out of doors, to be resolved

If Brutus so unkindly knocked, or no;

For Brutus, as you know, was Caesar's angel.

IN OTHER WORDS   Antony pretends to be reluctant to read the will, saying that he does not want to do wrong to Caesar's "honorable" killers. The crowd shouts out that the assassins are traitors and villains. Antony comes down off his platform and stands by Caesar's body. He tells the crowd to gather around, directing the crowd to make a circle around the body. Antony then shows them Caesar's torn, bloody cloak and describes the stabbing.

Judge, O you gods, how dearly Caesar loved him!

185 This was the most unkindest cut of all;

For when the noble Caesar saw him stab,

Ingratitude, more strong than traitors' arms,

Quite vanquished him. Then burst his mighty heart;

And, in his mantle muffling up his face,

190 Even at the base of Pompey's statue[23]

(Which all the while ran blood) great Caesar fell.

O, what a fall was there, my countrymen!

Then I, and you, and all of us fell down,

Whilst bloody treason flourished over us.

195 O, now you weep, and I perceive you feel

The dint[24] of pity; these are gracious drops.

---

21. **Nervii:** one of the tribes conquered by Caesar, in 57 B.C.
22. **envious** (EHN vee uhs): spiteful.
23. **statue:** pronounced in three syllables.
24. **dint:** stroke.

Kind souls, what weep you when you but behold

Our Caesar's vesture[25] wounded? Look you here,

Here is himself, marred as you see with traitors.

200   **First Plebeian.** O piteous spectacle!

Second Plebeian. O noble Caesar!

Third Plebeian. O woeful day!

Fourth Plebeian. O traitors, villains!

First Plebeian. O most bloody sight!

205   **Second Plebeian.** We will be revenged.

All. Revenge! About! Seek! Burn! Fire! Kill! Slay! Let not

a traitor live!

Antony. Stay, countrymen.

First Plebeian. Peace there! Hear the noble Antony.

210   **Second Plebeian.** We'll hear him, we'll follow him, we'll

die with him!

Antony.

Good friends, sweet friends, let me not stir you up

To such a sudden flood of mutiny.

They that have done this deed are honorable.

215   What private griefs[26] they have, alas, I know not,

That made them do it. They are wise and honorable,

And will, no doubt, with reasons answer you.

I come not, friends, to steal away your hearts;

I am no orator, as Brutus is;

220   But (as you know me all) a plain blunt man

That love my friend, and that they know full well

That gave me public leave to speak of him.

For I have neither writ, nor words, nor worth,

Action, nor utterance, nor the power of speech

225   To stir men's blood; I only speak right on.

I tell you that which you yourselves do know,

Show you sweet Caesar's wounds, poor poor dumb

mouths,

---

25. **vesture:** clothing.
26. **griefs:** grievances.

Your TURN

TRAGEDY

Some people think the moment when the mob turns on the assassins is the play's turning point. Why might this be the turning point?

_____

_____

_____

_____

Here's HOW

UNDERSTANDING PERSUASION

Brutus has already given the crowd his reasons for assassinating Caesar. In lines 215–217, Antony makes Brutus's high-minded reasons sound like they are only small and petty personal dislikes for Caesar.

Here's HOW

VOCABULARY

I looked up _dumb_ in a dictionary. The way it is used here (line 227), it means "can't talk" instead of "foolish" or "stupid."

**UNDERSTANDING
PERSUASION**

What does Antony say he would
do if he were Brutus (lines
228–232)?

_____

_____

_____

**UNDERSTANDING
PERSUASION**

In line 242, what final prop
does Antony display in order to
convince the plebeians that
they should turn against Brutus
and the other assassins?

_____

_____

_____

And bid them speak for me. But were I Brutus,

And Brutus Antony, there were an Antony

230 Would ruffle up your spirits, and put a tongue

In every wound of Caesar that would move

The stones of Rome to rise and mutiny.

All.

We'll mutiny.

First Plebeian. We'll burn the house of Brutus.

Third Plebeian.

Away, then! Come, seek the conspirators.

IN OTHER WORDS Antony says that what really killed
Caesar was not the daggers, but Caesar's sorrow at being
betrayed by his beloved Brutus. In a stirring speech, Antony
says that when Caesar fell, all Rome fell to the traitors that
plotted against him. The crowd shouts for revenge against
Caesar's killers. Antony claims to be a simple, plainspoken
man—not a skilled speechmaker, like Brutus.

Antony.

235 Yet hear me, countrymen. Yet hear me speak.

All.

Peace, ho! Hear Antony, most noble Antony!

Antony.

Why, friends, you go to do you know not what:

Wherein hath Caesar thus deserved your loves?

Alas, you know not; I must tell you then:

240 You have forgot the will I told you of.

All.

Most true, the will! Let's stay and hear the will.

Antony.

Here is the will, and under Caesar's seal.

To every Roman citizen he gives,

To every several[27] man, seventy-five drachmas.[28]

---

27. **several:** individual.
28. **drachmas** (DRAK muhz): silver coins (Greek currency).

Second Plebeian.

245   Most noble Caesar! We'll revenge his death!

Third Plebeian. O royal Caesar!

Antony. Hear me with patience.

All. Peace, ho!

Antony.

    Moreover, he hath left you all his walks,

250   His private arbors, and new-planted orchards,

    On this side Tiber; he hath left them you,

    And to your heirs forever: common pleasures,[29]

    To walk abroad and recreate yourselves.

    Here was a Caesar! When comes such another?

IN OTHER WORDS   The crowd is eager to rush off and punish the assassins. Antony tells them to wait and, at last, reads Caesar's will. The will states that Caesar has divided his fortune among the people of Rome. Each citizen is to receive seventy-five silver coins. In addition, Caesar has left his land as a public park for the people of Rome to enjoy.

First Plebeian.

255   Never, never! Come, away, away!

    We'll burn his body in the holy place,

    And with the brands fire the traitors' houses.

    Take up the body.

Second Plebeian. Go fetch fire.

260 **Third Plebeian.** Pluck down benches.

Fourth Plebeian. Pluck down forms, windows,[30] anything!

                    [*Exeunt* PLEBEIANS *with the body*.]

Antony.

    Now let it work: Mischief, thou art afoot,

    Take thou what course thou wilt.

Your TURN

VOCABULARY

The word *brands* in line 257 can mean "burned-on marks," "marks on cattle that show ownership," or "pieces of burning wood." Which meaning do you think it has here? Explain your answer.

_____

_____

_____

---

29. **common pleasures:** public recreation areas.
30. **forms, windows:** long benches and shutters.

[*Enter* SERVANT.]

How now, fellow?

Servant.

Sir, Octavius is already come to Rome.

265   **Antony.** Where is he?

Servant.

He and Lepidus are at Caesar's house.

Antony.

And thither will I straight to visit him;

He comes upon a wish. Fortune is merry,

And in this mood will give us anything.

Servant.

270   I heard him say, Brutus and Cassius

Are rid[31] like madmen through the gates of Rome.

Antony.

Belike[32] they had some notice of the people,

How I had moved them. Bring me to Octavius.

[*Exeunt.*]

IN OTHER WORDS   Now the mob rushes off to set fire to the houses of Caesar's killers. Antony is satisfied that he has accomplished what he set out to do. A servant enters and tells Antony that Octavius, Caesar's nephew, has arrived in Rome. Octavius brings the news that Brutus and Cassius have fled. Antony goes to visit Octavius.

---

31. **Are rid:** have ridden.
32. **Belike:** probably.

Persuasion

Persuasive speakers want to change the way their listeners think or to get their listeners to carry out an action. Here are the techniques they use:

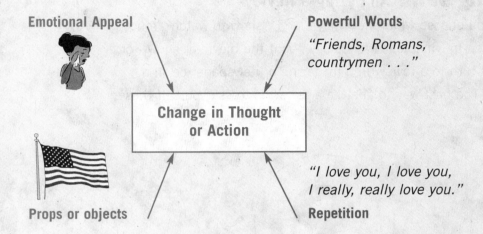

Emotional Appeal

Powerful Words

"Friends, Romans, countrymen . . ."

Change in Thought or Action

Props or objects

"I love you, I love you, I really, really love you."

Repetition

Read the elements from the play on the left-hand side of the chart below. Then, in the right-hand side, tell which persuasive techinque you think is used. One has been done for you.

Element from the Play	Persuasive Technique
1. Caesar's body	
2. the paper upon which is written Caesar's will	
3. the words: "Brutus is an honorable man" repeated three times in Antony's speech	
4. "Friends, Romans, countrymen . . ."	
5. the things in Caesar's will—his land which includes his walks, arbors, and orchards—given for the common pleasure of the people of Rome	Emotional Appeal: the Roman people will enjoy Caesar's gift of his land and be grateful to him.

Julius Caesar in an Absorbing Production

Reading Skill: Analyzing a Review

How do you choose which new movie or TV show to watch? You might listen to what your friends say about the movie or show—or you might turn to a review in a magazine or newspaper or on a Web site. The best way to analyze a review is to ask yourself these questions:

- Who is the reviewer? Is he or she qualified to write this review?
- What is the reviewer trying to get me to believe?
- What evidence—facts, examples, and critical judgments—does the reviewer use to back up his or her opinion?
- Does the reviewer cover everything? Does he or she leave out something I should know?

Into the Review

Orson Welles was an important figure in theater and film. His best-known movie, *Citizen Kane* (1941), has been called the most influential film in American movie history. John Mason Brown gave Welles's stage production of *Julius Caesar* a wonderful review, but not all critics shared his enthusiasm. Still, Welles's production ran for 157 performances in New York City—a record for a production of that play in the United States.

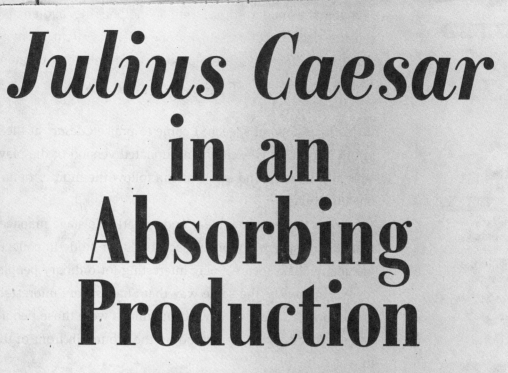

Julius Caesar
in an
Absorbing
Production

BASED ON THE REVIEW BY
John Mason Brown

Here's HOW

Your TURN

Your TURN

YOU NEED TO KNOW In 1937, Hitler was in power in Germany and Mussolini was dictator in Italy. It was a time of great world tension. On November 11 in that same year, the American director Orson Welles staged a modern-dress *Julius Caesar* at the Mercury Theater in New York City. Perhaps the modern-dress version helped the audience to see the rise of dictators in Europe in a new light. It might also have helped them rethink their own beliefs and values. This is the power of drama.

This is no funeral speech; I come to praise *Caesar*[1] at the Mercury, not to bury it. This exciting and updated version of the play tells the story of the harm and evil that can follow the murder of an all-powerful ruler.

5   Orson Welles's new ideas and remarkable stage management make Shakespeare no longer best suited for study in college. Welles has made Shakespeare's play interesting for ordinary people in today's audiences the same way that Shakespeare interested the groundlings in his own day. (Groundlings were those people who

10 bought cheap tickets and stood on the ground in front of the stage to watch the play.)

    The astonishing value of Mr. Welles's *Julius Caesar* is that it makes us look at the way nations, as well as men, behave. Mr. Welles has changed parts of the script,[2] but the meaning of the

15 drama is still there. The play may not be exactly the same as Shakespeare's tragedy;[3] however, it is about our present-day tragedy.[4]

---

1. **come to praise Caesar:** refers to Antony's speech in *The Tragedy of Julius Caesar,* Act III, Scene 2. In his funeral speech for Caesar, Antony says that he has come to bury Caesar, not to praise him.
2. **script** (skrihpt): the manuscript of a play or an actor's part in a play.
3. **tragedy** (TRAJ uh dee): a serious play that ends unhappily.
4. **tragedy:** a terrible happening; a calamity or disaster.

Mr. Welles sets *Julius Caesar* on a simple, bare stage, with only brick walls, a few steps, and a platform under lights that create
20 shadows and deep empty spaces. That is all, and it is all that is needed.

Mr. Welles directs the actors in creative ways and uses sound—such as the herdlike thunder of the mob's feet—effectively. The play's characters are well thought out and excellently performed. As Brutus,
25 Mr. Welles shows his gift for speaking great words simply. George Coulouris, as Antony, makes the words "Friends, Romans, countrymen" sound fresh and natural. Joseph Holland's Caesar is an imperious[5] dictator[6] who could be seen in today's news programs.

Mr. Welles and his actors have achieved a triumph that is
30 exceptional[7] from almost every point of view.

—from the *New York Post,*
November 12, 1937

Your TURN

ANALYZING A REVIEW

Re-read lines 22–28. Then, give one piece of evidence—a fact, example, or judgment—that the reviewer uses to back up his opinion that this is an excellent production.

_____

_____

_____

_____

Here's HOW

ANALYZING A REVIEW

This review was published in the *New York Post*. That seems to be a pretty important paper, so I guess I can trust this reviewer to be truthful.

---

5. **imperious** (ihm PIHR ee uhs): overbearing; domineering; arrogant.
6. **dictator** (DIHK tay tuhr): all-powerful ruler; a ruler who is not elected but seizes control of a government.
7. **exceptional** (ehk SEHP shuh nuhl): unusual.

Analyzing a Review

Answer the questions below. One has been done for you.

1. What does the reviewer want you to believe about this production of *Julius Caesar*?

   Brown wants me to believe that this production is good. He also wants me to believe that

   his opinion is correct.

   _____

2. Do you think John Mason Brown is qualified to write this review? Why or why not?

   _____

   _____

   _____

3. Give one detail about the play that the reviewer uses to back up his opinion.

   _____

   _____

   _____

4. What else would you like to know about the play?

   _____

   _____

   _____

5. Would you have gone to see this play? Why or why not?

   _____

   _____

   _____